THE
LAST
LAUGH

STEVE LEGG

'Shocked would be an understatement when Steve told me of his prognosis, but I promised I'd walk the cancer journey alongside him. We have regular catch-ups and prayer sessions, and as we reminisce over old stories we always end up crying with laughter! Steve's so positive, and if I didn't know about the medics' discovery, I would not know there was anything wrong with him. Only God knows our futures, but nothing seems to stop Steve enjoying the life he loves living.'
Ishmael, singer-songwriter, speaker and author

'What a blessing and an encouragement it is to know Steve. His attitude following an incredibly difficult diagnosis has been an example to us all. Far from denial or mere glass-half-full positivity, he has deployed his faith, leaned into his relationships and served faithfully wherever possible. There are lessons to be learned from those who have walked tough paths, and I have certainly learned a lot from Steve. These nuggets of wisdom are sure to encourage many.'
Cathy Madavan, author and speaker

'If you were stuck on a desert island and could only have a dozen people with you, you would want Steve Legg to be one of them. Steve – and therefore this book – is a fabulous and rare mixture of quick-witted humour, spontaneous joy and zest for life, as well as being deeply reflective, sensitive and insightful. His last challenging chapter has shown his true colours, which shine as brightly as ever!'
Simon Guillebaud, author and speaker

'When one of your greatest and closest mates in all the world calls to tell you he's been given five months to live, the world stands still for a moment. Only a brief moment, though, because this is no ordinary bloke, and within a short time Steve was talking faith, hope, life and love with his characteristic optimism and humour. Since receiving the news I have laughed until tears ran down my cheeks recording podcasts and chatting over food, and have privately shed a tear as I've prayed for him and his beautiful family. Steve, being who he is, even takes time to cheer me on in my own health battles. A remarkable man. Anything he has to say is worth your time. It'll encourage and bless you no end.'

Carl Beech, leader of Edge Ministries, president of Christian Vision for Men (CVM) and founder of The Gathering

'When Steve got his life-limiting cancer diagnosis, he initially responded in a way we probably all would. As he says himself, there were a lot of tears. And then this remarkable man made a decision. A decision to live, to enjoy his life and to thank God for every moment he has left. It's a powerful thing to see, because it reminds us it's the way we should all be living anyway. Steve continues to defy the medical predictions, and I for one will keep cheering on this lovely, inspiring, faith-filled man.'

Tim Vine, author and comedian

'I read the manuscript in one sitting. It made me laugh and cry, seconds apart. It's so honest it hurts. Every chapter taught me an important lesson, and I am not the same.'

Debra Green OBE, founder of Redeeming Our Communities (ROC)

'Comedy gigs, a cartoon, sixteen books and launching a men's magazine. There's nothing this man can't do – including, it seems, beating the timeframe of a stage-four cancer prognosis and continuing to change the world through laughter at the same time. The book is a treat, and so is the man. If you need a perspective reboot, read it.'

Philippa Hanna, singer-songwriter

'Steve Legg has entertained thousands with his wit, humour and stunning illusions. But this professional entertainer is also a man of deep faith. I warmly commend this account of how that faith holds him fast in times of enormous personal challenge.'

Revd Ian Coffey, author and speaker

'I've always loved and admired Steve and Bekah. This year, that love has soared as we have journeyed – together with so many of their friends and family – along their toughest-ever road. Their unwavering faith and ability to communicate their beliefs, even in the midst of deep pain and suffering, is nothing short of beautiful.

Steve's words here are expressed with humour, hope and a lightness of spirit that is delightfully typical of them both. This story is truly a testament that no matter where we are, Jesus is there with us. Its pages show the inspiring and authentic progress of people who refuse to live reduced, self-referential lives, even when told that life as they know it could be ending.

An engaging read throughout, these chapters will lead you to the most wonderful of all conclusions: that we are never, ever alone, and never, ever forsaken. Hope. Heart. Humour. Humanity. This gripping story has everything.'

Ems Hancock, author and speaker

'Steve is an extraordinary person, a man full of life and vigour. He's an entertainer, an entrepreneur and a fun-filled character refreshingly devoid of ego, yet most of all a lover of God. As you read through the narrative of these pages, I guarantee that, like me, you'll be inspired and provoked. In the face of such a stark and negative prognosis, Steve and Bekah's resilience and honesty shine through. Raw and real, this is a true journey of faith.'

Dave Bilbrough, songwriter and author

'I've been close friends with Steve for more than thirty years, and we have shared many adventures as co-workers in God's great harvest field. His warmth, courage and humour throughout this journey with cancer have been nothing short of inspirational. As I write this, he continues to defy the odds, riding a wave of prayer power generated by thousands of people who love him.'

Steve Lee, filmmaker and evangelist

'*The Last Laugh* is a remarkable book. Once I started it, I couldn't put it down – laughing, brushing away a tear and going on a journey with Steve, the funny man, as he faced the no-joke reality of the diagnosis of a terminal illness. But this is not just Steve's story; he draws lessons that can change not only the way we view our death – but also our life.'

Rob Parsons OBE, author of *The Heart of Success*

'"Family of choice" is what I call Steve and Bekah. They're the "in it and mean it" type of friends, scaffolding many of us with love, loyalty and humour. These past months since Steve's diagnosis we've had conversations you never expect to have with your "youngish" mates… yet the candour, the bravery and the willingness to sit in the unknown and mystery-in-faith, with all that Steve and the family is facing, has been extraordinary. A one-in-a-million man.'

Tarn Bright, author, speaker and CEO of Home for Good

'I've been privileged to journey with Steve over the years, working together on stage and page. He's a dear friend and a total inspiration. You will see through this memoir that his character is as colourful as his shirts, and when it comes to bringing magic to life he doesn't miss a trick. Steve is a living reminder that, through faith, anything – even something as horrific as terminal cancer – can be turned to good.'

Tony Vino, author and comedian

'To say that Steve Legg is a unique, one-of-a-kind person is an understatement. I am in awe of the way he has approached a life-changing diagnosis with his characteristic down-to-earth attitude and an overwhelmingly heavenly perspective. Well known for making people laugh, the Steve in this book will also make you cry, provoke and challenge you to your core, and cause you to break out in wild applause.'

Sue Rinaldi, author and singer-songwriter

'*The Last Laugh* delivers everything its title promises, and then more! I've never read any other book like it. Ever. It was impossible to put down. At this most painful of moments in his life, Steve Legg's plain-talking honesty, wit, wisdom and depth of faith are as profound, practical, challenging and life-affirming as it gets. As he puts it himself, there are no easy answers, only good responses.'

Steve Chalke MBE, author, speaker and founder of Oasis Charitable Trust

THE
LAST
LAUGH

Reflections of a funnyman with terminal cancer

STEVE LEGG

scm

Dedication
(that's what you need...)

To my beautiful first granddaughter, Marla. The jury was out as to whether we'd ever get to meet, but we did. I'm so grateful you arrived, and that I was here to see it.

I hope your old Pops gets to share many of the world's wonders with you. I can't wait to introduce you to the joys of The Repair Shop *and strolls along the beach, and to take you to my favourite Indian restaurant for your first curry.*

I hope I'm here to help you enjoy exploring this wonderful experience called life. And never forget, it's always better with Jesus by your side.

'All we have to decide is what to do with the
time that is given to us.'

Gandalf in J. R. R. Tolkien's *The Fellowship of the Ring*

Contents

Acknowledgements

They say teamwork makes the dream work. It's true. This book would never have happened without my amazing, kind, talented and generous friends: Dr Mark Stibbe, Tony Vino, Bob Crowther, Joy Tibbs, Esther Kotecha, Rob Parsons OBE, Peter Meadows, Andrew Saunders at Halcyon, Mark and Helen Johnson, and my greatest supporter, the legend and profound inspiration that is my wife, Bekah. She's walked every step of this journey with me. I wouldn't be here without her. Thanks a million.

Foreword

It was one of those 'Is this God speaking to me?' moments that many followers of Jesus experience. A thought surfaces, seemingly from nowhere, and its persistent luminosity makes us wonder if the Holy Spirit is broadcasting on our personal wavelength. Some believers insist their lives are punctuated with daily, even hourly, revelations. I haven't found God to be quite so chatty. So when I do sense his nudge, I usually dash into crisis mode. Is this thought racing around my mind just my wishful thinking, is it truly the divine voice, or is it merely the aftereffects of last night's chicken tikka masala? I wish God would speak with a louder, clearer voice, but perhaps he whispers because he wants us to draw closer, that we might hear.

Back to my inner nudge. Halfway through a Sunday morning service, I was just about to preach when the thought surfaced again: 'Take a look at my beautiful people.'

So I did.

I looked around at the sea of faces that was our congregation, and recalled some of their stories. Over there was John, who married after desperately longing for a soulmate for decades, only to lose his darling in a drunk-driver-caused crash. Towards the back was Sally, who had poured her heart out on a lonely mission field. Not many responded to her life of kingdom service, but she stayed the course until retirement. Now she feels somewhat lost, surplus to requirements. I look her way but she is unaware, for her eyes are shut tight, her hands raised in worship. Beautiful indeed.

And the whisper confirmed the truth that God who flings stars into being with a word, daubs drab skies with rainbows and paints deep sea fishes in stunning colours that no human eye will ever see – this God of ours finds the greatest delight when he sees hearts that trust him through mystery.

In recent months, I have pondered yet another dazzling sight. Our dear friend Steve has been given a terminal cancer diagnosis. A tearful oncologist delivered the dreaded news that he had just months to live. There are hopeful possibilities with some radical treatment options, but he, Bekah and the whole family are treading a bewildering path: the remote possibility of a medical solution and their belief in a miracle-working God who can heal in a moment, all entwined with a visit to a hospice to discuss end-of-life care.

But Steve and Bekah have decided. Even when life is threatened, it still goes on. The weekend after the dark diagnosis, Steve, a brilliant evangelist who uses comedy in his Tricks and Laughs presentations, performed at four outreach events. He is also the publisher of *Sorted*, an outstanding Christian magazine for men. Bekah continues to lead Restored, a non-profit dedicated to helping victims of domestic abuse.

Recently, during a transatlantic phone chat, Bekah spoke of some of the good things they are celebrating, even as they pass through the valley of the shadow. 'There is so much beauty to be seen, even in this horrible season,' she said. 'We don't want to miss the lovely things that God is surely doing.'

That's when we had to pause for tears because, in celebrating treasure that can be found even in darkness, Bekah and Steve have themselves become quite beautiful in their persistent faith and faithfulness. In the intense and unwelcome roller-coaster ride that suffering brings, they are clinging to God through the white-knuckle ride. They are, in short, a stunning sight.

Often we focus on what's wrong with the world and with the Church. Fixated on the failures of high-profile Christian leaders, we sink into despair. Preoccupied with the picky pettiness that breaks out when someone suggests moving the pews, we wonder if there's any future for a people so resistant to change.

But all around us today, there are quiet yet glorious examples of tenacious dedication. If you're one of them, know this: your love for Christ surely turns his head.

In this warm, authentic book that is rich in wisdom and void of cliché, you will find hope and inspiration. As you trace Steve's journey, you'll peer into the shadowland of suffering and discover that the light of Jesus shines brightly there.

As you read, please say a prayer for Steve and Bekah, and their lovely family.

And if you're preoccupied with ugliness – in yourself, in others, in our broken world and imperfect Church – then know this: there's beauty to be found in the most surprising places.

Go on. Turn the page, and look again.

Jeff Lucas, author, speaker and broadcaster
Colorado, USA

Prologue

It's the film most often voted number one in the top-ten movies of all time by viewers and critics alike. I'm talking about *The Shawshank Redemption*. You will almost certainly be familiar with it, so I don't need to say any more than that it's a story based on one of Stephen King's tales about prisoners who leave their mark on the institutions in which they're incarcerated.

In the case of *Shawshank* (as it's affectionately known), the film focuses on a man called Andy (Tim Robbins) who is wrongfully arrested, charged, sentenced, and then imprisoned for the murder of his wife and her lover.

In prison, his life is improved by the formation of a friendship with Red (Morgan Freeman). In many ways, *Shawshank* is a buddy movie, and part of its appeal is its celebration of an unlikely friendship between two men – one white, the other black.

There are so many famous quotes in *Shawshank*, some of which have entered our everyday vocabulary. One of the best-known and loved is the word of wisdom uttered by Andy and remembered later by his friend Red, which goes something like this: 'We all have a choice. We have to get busy doing one of two things: living or dying.' I would also add laughing or crying here. If you're going to busy yourself with living, then busy yourself with laughing as well.

That's the choice every inmate of Shawshank State Prison has.

They can either choose to accept the situation and find ways to live rather than merely exist, to thrive rather than merely survive, or they can give in to the despair that surrounds them on every side, like the walls of their cells.

Andy chooses to busy himself with living.

As does Red.

This book is about the two-year journey I've been on since I received that initial news, then that the cancer had spread to multiple locations in my body, and later that I had only five months to live.

That was a kind of sentence.

Some of you may think it was a death sentence.

Later in this book, I'll tell you otherwise.

I chose to get busy living, not dying.

I chose to get busy laughing, not crying.

And I also chose to get busy writing.

1

The phone call

One in two of us will get cancer in our lifetime.

Guess which one of those two I am?

I had no idea one Thursday afternoon that I was a phone call away from my life being turned upside-down. It was 18 November 2021, a year and a half into the Covid pandemic. At this stage in my life I had been on the road for thirty-three years (you know what the traffic's like on the M25), using a mix of comedy, trickery and mystery to communicate the Christian message to young and old. It had taken me to twenty-one countries across the world, but all of that was on hold because of the repeated lockdowns. I so missed sharing the good news and hearing people laugh. I had only been able to do a few Zoom gigs and car park shows. It just wasn't the same.

It was 5:15 p.m., and I was relaxing in front of *The Chase*, my favourite TV quiz show, with a big mug of coffee. I was watching members of the public take on some of the greatest quizzers in the country: the Beast, the Vixen, the Governess, the Dark Destroyer, the Sinnerman and the latest addition to the Chasers' team, the Menace. I'm a creature of habit, a lover of routine, so I was enjoying watching host Bradley Walsh banter with the contestants, as I had hundreds of times in the past. I was joining in, answering most of the questions. This day, Big Leggy, the Leggend, was on fire.

And then my phone rang.

It was the dermatologist I had visited two weeks earlier. He told me the results were in, and the spot he'd done a biopsy on was 'a little bit of skin cancer'. I was shocked, but as he continued to speak, he shared something hopeful. 'We should be able to get rid of it.'

The next day, Friday, was my wife Bekah's graduation. I was so proud of her and all the hard work she'd put into her MA, and was looking forward to celebrating with her and a couple of our daughters at Christchurch Priory. I decided not to tell her straightaway because I didn't want to spoil her special day. I would tell her afterwards, once we got home. But when she finished her work call and came into the sitting room at 5:30 p.m., she could tell from the look on my face that something was wrong. It was at this point I realised I'd make a terrible poker player!

She asked what the matter was. I told her I'd heard from the dermatologist, and passed on what he'd said about me having 'a little bit of skin cancer'.

I shared with Bekah the rest of what the medic had said. Normally in challenging situations, she is the worrier and I'm the one who's more chilled. What was concerning on this occasion was the way the roles were reversed. Bekah wasn't unduly concerned. She knew there were different kinds of skin cancer, and that most are nothing to worry about. The dermatologist's description convinced her that this was what we were dealing with in my case.

That night, she slept like a baby.

I, on the other hand, felt less calm. I had a restless night, tossing and turning, imagining different scenarios and fearing the worst. The only thing that calmed me down was watching Bekah sleep deeply and peacefully all night long. Her response reassured me that maybe everything would be okay.

As it turned out, I was right to be worried. And later, when we became aware of the full extent of my diagnosis and prognosis, she reflected that her initial lack of concern would come back to bite her. We'll come to that in due course.

In life, questions are asked that are far heavier and graver than the ones posed by Bradley Walsh on *The Chase*. Perhaps one of the biggies is this: how would you react if a doctor called to say that you had cancer?

Given the experience of many British people during the pandemic, when it was practically impossible to get any kind of doctor's appointment, your first reaction might be to pass out with shock that you were actually speaking to one. Maybe you would go on to sense something altogether less flippant – the seismic shock of hearing the 'c' word applied to your life. Maybe you'd feel dizzy or disorientated, as if your whole world was tilting on an axis you'd always thought of as stable, secure, steadfast. Maybe you'd be in denial. Perhaps you'd feel afraid.

How would you respond if it was the Dark Destroyer of cancer pursuing you, as opposed to *The Chase*'s Shaun Wallace?

What if the chase was not about outwitting a quizmaster, but responding in a courageous way to a devastating diagnosis?

Would you answer that question well?

Or would you answer it poorly?

Would you get busy living?

Or would you get busy dying?

Our lives are full of questions, some of them trivial, others life-altering. Whether we are standing in front of a crowd and performing (as I do) or sitting down in front of the TV and watching a quiz show (as I also do), most of us never imagine we're just one phone call away from receiving news that will send shockwaves through our ordinary world and send us into a new landscape of healing, hospitals and even a visit to a hospice.

The truth is, life is precious and life is fragile, and we can never know what is only a phone call away.

While I was writing this book, I remembered a time during the early 1980s when a famous Anglican preacher called David Watson was confronted by such a challenge. He was on the road a lot, just as I am. Then he received some bad news, just as I did. He was told he had terminal cancer, just as I was.

Fear no Evil: One man deals with terminal illness (H. Shaw Publishers, 1985) is one of the first Christian books I ever read and the last book David Watson ever wrote (and he wrote some real classics). It's the diary of the last year of his life. In the Introduction, he described the aftermath of hearing his prognosis. He talked about the fears this news stirred in his heart, and the questions he had to grapple with in his mind. Perhaps the biggest question of all was why a God who is love would allow him to suffer in this way. In response to that question – perhaps the most difficult of all questions – he had this to say:

The problem of suffering is always a baffling one, devoid of simple solutions, and yet the experience of that suffering is all around us. The question is, how can we live with it, face it, overcome it, and reach that position where we *fear no evil*?

As he drew nearer and nearer to death, Watson wrote something utterly profound and practical in response to the biggest question of all: the one about why we suffer. He explains that there are no easy answers, only good responses.

We all search for compelling answers to complex questions. But life is not a maths exam, and sometimes there are no answers. Sometimes all we can do is say that we don't know why, but we are going to try to respond to a life-altering problem in a good way before our final papers are handed in.

That's what David Watson exhorted us to do.

I think I can relate to that.

I'm not going to try to answer the big question about why God has permitted this horrible illness in my life. What I am going to do is suggest some good responses. Those responses have come from many hours of deep soul searching, so I promise I will not give you pat answers or meaningless phrases like, 'If life gives you lemons, make lemonade.' In my experience, homemade lemonade is always bitter and disappointing.

My first suggestion is this: get busy living.

That's not an easy answer, but it is a good response.

It's a good response when your Chaser is cancer.

Sometimes we give daft responses to standard questions. Poor old Bradley Walsh has had to endure some unbelievable answers to the questions he's posed on *The Chase*.

One time, he asked a contestant which breed of Peking bird might be found in a well-known Chinese appetiser. The answer given was not duck, as expected, but parrot.

Another contestant was asked which Scottish city Dundonians would be from. The answer given? Cardiff!

On another occasion, Bradley asked a young lad who had been studying medicine for six years which organ the pituitary gland was in. Instead of correctly identifying the brain, the student answered that it was in the neck.

All I can say is, if I ever end up having brain surgery, I hope he's not the one operating on me. That would be a real pain in the neck!

In the meantime, I've decided to go for good responses.

2

Our blended family

Bekah is not just my wife. She's my best friend, my confidante and my greatest supporter. I genuinely don't know where I would have been without her, especially during my health challenges of the last two years.

We met on holiday. My three girls and I had been going to Le Pas Opton in France for years – a beautiful four-star campsite run by Spring Harvest in the Vendée region on the Atlantic coast. The kids loved hanging out there, and I could read my books by the pool knowing they were safe. That year, the view was enhanced by a cutie sitting across the pool from me. She was wearing a sky-blue bikini.

Before I share more, a confession. One of the toughest things I've ever had to do is accept the failure of my first marriage. I had been determined to make it work – not to give up, not to lose my children and my wife, not to become a divorcé.

I know countless people have felt this, but as a Christian, and particularly as a full-time evangelist, I felt the pressure to succeed in my marriage even more keenly. In the end, there wasn't anything I could do when my wife told me she'd had enough and asked me to leave. Short of handcuffing myself to the banisters and refusing, which even I could see wasn't the answer, I had to go. I was a professional escapologist back in the day, but this was one fix I couldn't get myself out of. So I became a single dad for five years.

There we were – Amber (eleven), Emmie (eight) and little Maddie (just about to turn six) – enjoying our hols in sunny France, when I first clapped eyes on Bekah. She was stretched out in the sun attempting to top up her tan, and there was a small blonde child lying on her tummy. With her free hand she was playing Ludo with her other daughter. I was more than a little taken, particularly as it appeared that she was on holiday with her mum, and this was single-parent family week. I had come away with my neighbours, Scott and Martine, and their two boys. Martine took it upon herself to investigate.

Judging by the puzzled look on Bekah's face, Martine was being subtle, if a little odd. My neighbour soon returned to report that there was no wedding ring to be seen. This was interesting news, though I was possibly more intrigued to see what kind of a tan line you end up sporting when sunbathing with a little girl lying on you.

The week continued without incident. The children were happy, I was happy, and the weather was good. All of us were slowly turning into little brown berries under the blazing sun. Maddie overcame her fear of the water and started to swim. I became king of the campsite barbecue, inviting friends, camping neighbours and complete strangers to share our burgers and sausages.

Meanwhile, the foxy woman remained elusive.

She was a no-show at the single parents' wine-and-cheese evening. I had to enjoy the wonderful spread Care for the Family's team, Robin and Cathy, had produced without her company.

The debate continues to this day as to who made the first move.

Bekah says, 'The whole Martine checking me out thing renders the argument over before it's begun.'

I disagree.

I could no sooner have stopped Martine launching her Cupid mission than I could have stopped the sun rising.

In any case, on the last night of my holiday, Bekah chatted me up at the bar and I invited her to join our team in the quiz. We sat and nattered, exchanged phone numbers, and agreed to meet up if I should ever be down her way. It just so happened I was going to be down her way a fortnight later.

I spent a long time trying to convince Bekah that we lived too far apart to date, but I contacted her most days anyway. In return, she told me I was stupid to think that distance mattered until the day I realised she was right. I *was* stupid, and distance only matters while you are apart. So I phoned her and asked her to marry me, to help solve the distance problem. It wasn't quite the proposal every girl dreams of – down on one knee with red roses at the top of the Eiffel Tower. I think it came as such a surprise that she nearly dropped the phone. But it worked. At least I hadn't popped the question via text. I faxed it instead (joke).

Let's face it, it can be a big enough challenge to find someone who can love you. Then, if you are a Christian, you also need someone who will love God. And as single parents we needed a third thing – to love each other's kids.

A triple whammy.

Bekah was right all along. She often is. I had met the perfect woman for me. She was, and is, everything I could ever want: beautiful, clever, funny and kind, and most importantly she loves God. She also loves me and my girls. That's not an easy combo to find.

It had taken me ten months to recognise that I would go any distance for this woman and her girls, so a walk down the aisle was a no-brainer. It took just four to close the gap, get married and start our journey together.

Our wedding was a joyful day. On the only sunny Saturday in August, we were wed in her parents' back garden. We tied the knot in the presence of our friends and family, but most importantly in front of our girls. This celebration wasn't just about me and Bekah; it was about all of us. The girls still refer to it as 'the day *we* got married'. They consider it their day, too.

And it truly was.

They even came on our honeymoon!

We all went to a lovely hotel in Jersey and began the process of becoming one family. The girls quickly became a little gang that outnumbered the grown-ups. Every night in their hotel room felt like a sleepover. We all had a blast. It was a great way to start our new family life.

When we came home, we established the routines that all blended families know. Some of the kids shared their time between our home and their mum's. We would go on to face all the challenges that come with the complexities of second marriages and combined families, but that first week together provided a good foundation and wonderful memories as we got to know one another.

I should add that we did have a proper honeymoon –just the two of us – a few months later, in Bermuda of all places. We won it in a competition, so it didn't cost us a penny! We even got upgraded both ways on the plane, courtesy of some pals of mine at BA.

It's fair to say that, as a family, we are blended. And we are blessed.

3

No time to lose

On 3 December 2021, I visited Dr Khan, a senior consultant dermatologist and co-clinical lead of the Dermatology department at Southlands Hospital in Shoreham-by-Sea. This was the man who would deal with the cancer we thought was fairly innocuous.

It was the first of many new hospitals for us – a tired, low-lying building with a long corridor, which of course meant we were right down at the other end. I took a socially distanced and recently sanitised seat, and watched a gardening show on the tiny TV until it was my turn to go in.

Bekah wasn't with me for this appointment. She had been away with work the night before and was heading down to Devon. I agreed that I would call her on speaker phone during the appointment so she could hear the news straight from the horse's mouth and ask all the questions I wouldn't have thought to ask.

I was called in by a nurse, and then another nurse entered the consultation room.

'The doctor will be with you in a few moments,' she said.

'Please strip down to your underwear.'

I was a little puzzled by this, because the doctor was meant to be looking at my foot.

'You do work here, don't you?' I asked. I needed to check she wasn't asking random men to strip off just to get her kicks. She laughed. I breathed a sigh of relief that it wasn't laundry day in the Legg household, so I wasn't going commando.

I was still feeling a little apprehensive, so I took the opportunity to visit the men's toilets while I waited to meet Dr Khan. I was horrified when I realised I had a small wet patch on the front of my underpants after I'd finished.

Never one to want to show myself up, I set about fixing the problem. Stopping to check that no one was around, I positioned myself in front of a hand dryer and got the hot air blowing to dry my pants out. I was particularly glad it was an old-school dryer rather than a Dyson Airblade, or I would have had to climb into it – which I don't think is anatomically possible. Either way, I'm so glad no one walked in.

Having solved my issue (pun intended), I got to meet Dr Khan for the first of many times. He was friendly, but curt and to the point. Bekah had joined the conversation at the other end of the phone by this point.

'I'm frustrated that the biopsy isn't as clear as I'd like,' he said. *You and me both*, I thought.

'It doesn't reveal what kind of cancer it is. Rather than have another biopsy, I want you to return as a matter of urgency to have it removed. We can then do some more tests.'

For Bekah, these words set off alarm bells for the first time. This wasn't quite what she'd thought we were dealing with. The note of urgency caused us both some anxiety.

Dr Khan said he wanted me to come back in the next couple of days. The clear message was that there was no time to waste.

'I'm going to remove the tumour,' he said. 'I'll take a 2mm margin. Let's hope that's all that's needed.' He explained that the depth of the tumour would be significant. 'The deeper the tumour, the deeper the problem.'

Then he talked about recovery. 'You'll have to take it easy,' he said. 'In other words, do nothing. You'll need to take time off work.'

'I can't do that, Doc,' I said. 'I'm self-employed. This is my busiest season. I can't let people down.'

But Dr Khan was adamant. 'You're not to walk any distance for three weeks. You won't be able to drive. And you'll have to elevate your foot to aid the healing.'

I was literally being told to take my foot off the gas, and it was finally beginning to sink in, big time. This was more serious than either of us had thought.

A week later, Dr Khan began the procedure to remove the melanoma on the underside of my foot. I knew the injection would hurt; I'd had one before. This is a very sensitive part of the body. It was so painful when I had the initial biopsy that I almost kicked my new dermatologist pal in the head.

Jean-Claude Van Damme eat your heart out.

'Don't worry,' I said. 'I've prepared myself for the injection.'

Dr Khan looked concerned. 'I'm afraid to say I'm going to have to give you *four* injections this time to numb the area.'

My face dropped.

Bekah had come with me this time. She held my leg down during the jabs so I didn't kick this good doctor in the face. He got to work and cut out the bad stuff, and then she watched him sew me up. All the while she kept her feelings hidden. After the doctor was finished, she listened to the nurse's instructions about caring for the wound. It was Level 101 in what was to become quite a wound-care training programme for her.

I was still insistent that I'd be fine walking, but it swiftly became apparent as we left to head back to the car that this was not going to be as easy as I had thought.

First, it hurt.

Second, it bled.

All this meant that Bekah had to apply her new lessons straightaway to stem the flow.

In the end, I had to stop and wait while she went to the car to bring it closer to the entrance. 'They should have given you crutches,' she muttered.

On the way home we called Daphne, my mother-in-law. If Bekah has been my rock throughout this ordeal, then Daphne has been a very large pebble. If Bekah has been my bridge over troubled waters, Daphne has been the pleasant tea shop at the side of the crossing. What I'm trying to say is that she's pretty amazing, and as an ex-nurse and cancer survivor herself, she's been through more medical dramas than George Clooney in *ER*. She's a walking, talking *Gray's Anatomy* – and what she doesn't know about medical matters she makes up for in calm reasoning.

As ever, she listened, asked lots of questions and reassured us, and we drove back to Littlehampton feeling a lot more positive. When I got in, I sat down to enjoy *The Repair Shop* with homemade shepherd's pie and a large glass of Pinot Grigio. The first month of rest had begun. My lockdown had turned into a lock-in.

But this was easier said than done. I felt guilty about cancelling all my December gigs. I hated disappointing people, and it was tough financially. The churches that were due to host me were very understanding. All bar one (which asked for the £100 deposit back) were happy to reschedule. Being asked to return that money was a bit of a blow, but it was completely understandable.

Bekah found it scary, too. With Christmas coming, and my income disappearing, she was worried about how we would manage. We don't have financial reserves; we've always lived one month to the next and trusted God to provide. That approach was being put to the test.

Before we really had time to think about this shortfall, a cheque came in from someone who knew nothing about the cancer, and it covered all three weeks of lost income. Within a couple of days, the same amount arrived again. God was very good.

I was still incapacitated, so Bekah had to walk our dog, Colbie, as well as doing all her other extra chores. One day, as she strolled along the beach with Colbie, she thanked God for his goodness and generosity. He had provided above and beyond what we needed.

As she prayed, she remembered the storehouses Joseph had prepared at God's bidding to prepare for the years of famine to come. Maybe we'd received extra because we were going to need extra. Maybe I was going to be off my feet for longer than we thought.

That was bittersweet. Like homemade lemonade.

We recognised that God had been faithful and kind, but we also realised he might be preparing us for a longer journey than we'd hoped.

The dressing stayed on for a week, and this meant a week without showers in a bid to keep it dry. After five days I was ready for a good wash, but Bekah put her foot down – something I literally couldn't do. We wondered if I could manage a bath, but the reality is, I'm a tall, clumsy man, and I did not have the dexterity required to get in and out on one foot.

The bandage didn't come off easily after all that bleeding, but when it did, Bekah showed me a photograph. The original spot they had removed was no more than half a centimetre in diameter. I was certainly not prepared for the three-inch scar that reached from between my big toe and the next one to the centre of my foot. That was impressive.

Bekah was a trooper. She instantly set about cleaning the wound, which made it look significantly less horrible.

I was glad not to be walking on it so I could give it a chance to heal. But the healing process wasn't straightforward, as there isn't much slack in the skin on your feet. The wound pulled, gaped and occasionally bled. The stitches had to stay in for three weeks.

The dressings stayed on much longer.

I was determined to get back on my feet in time to cook Christmas lunch. It was a quiet affair with our girls – another Covid Christmas – but I'm usually chief of the weekly Sunday roast with all the trimmings, and I wanted to give Bekah a treat after watching her do literally everything single-handedly for three weeks. I wanted her to watch me do something single-footedly for one day. She definitely deserved it.

The week before Christmas, Dr Khan explained that his fears had been realised and the melanoma was more than 3.1mm deep. That meant more surgery – a wider, deeper excision – with a 2cm margin this time, and some lymph nodes taken out to see if the melanoma had spread.

Lymph nodes are part of the lymphatic system. This is a network of thin tubes and nodes that carry a clear fluid called lymph around the body. They're an important part of the immune system, and play a vital role in fighting infection and destroying old or abnormal cells. The nodes are bean-shaped structures that filter the lymph fluid and trap bacteria, viruses and cancer cells.

Dr Khan broke the news: 'You have acral lentiginous melanoma. It's usually found on the palms of the hands and soles of the feet, or around the big toenail. It can also grow under the nails. It's nothing to do with exposure to the sun. It's a rogue gene that's caused this, and it's also very rare. Only five to ten out of every one hundred people diagnosed with melanoma have this type. Unfortunately, it's also a particularly aggressive form of melanoma.'

This type of melanoma is most common in dark-skinned people, yet I had it. I always like to buck a trend, but we hoped it hadn't gone too deep or spread elsewhere in my body. Only one per cent of skin cancer sufferers get it on their foot. I'm one of them. Another was Bob Marley. I like to think it was after he received treatment that he wrote 'Get Up, Stand Up'.

Dr Khan referred us to his colleague, Mr Sharma, at the Queen

Victoria Hospital in the heart of East Grinstead, a relic from the Second World War specialising in plastic surgery. It originally opened so that surgeons could respond to the horrors of war inflicted on soldiers. The main hospital is an old and dilapidated building, but the names of its wards and rooms are a nod to timeless and glorious days: the Spitfire Restaurant, Lancaster Lounge, Canadian Wing and Hurricane Café. Instead of keys to open locks, each door uses an enigma code. Well not quite, but you get the idea.

Mr Sharma is a consultant – a plastic, reconstructive and cosmetic surgeon who specialises in skin cancer. He trained in sentinel node biopsy and the surgical management of patients with advanced melanoma. He was definitely the right man for the job.

By this point Covid restrictions were back in force, so Bekah dropped me at the door. She wrapped herself up in a blanket and sat in the car with her laptop – the very definition of a mobile office – trying to keep on top of her work while she waited. Fortunately, we had a very kind nurse called Julie who gave her a call and let her in, duly masked, which meant we would both hear the explanation of what was about to come next.

'There'll be a three-month recovery time,' she said.

Julie couldn't see much of our masked faces, but she could tell that we were shocked. She explained that if I was having the equivalent surgery almost anywhere else on my body it would be a few weeks, but the foot is complicated. The lack of slack skin means you can't just pull the skin in and close it around the wound. The 2cm margin around and below the scar from the last surgery would leave a big hole that needed to be filled. That would be done with a 'mesh' – essentially, a biological sponge that would act like a scaffolding so I could regain some padding on the bottom of my foot and be able to walk.

She concluded: 'After a month, if that heals well, the surgeon will do a skin graft to cover it up. That will take six weeks to heal

– hopefully well enough so you can walk on it gently.'

I did some calculations, trying to work out where in the year I could afford to take that much time off work.

Bekah was very quiet.

When Mr Sharma came in, I asked, 'Can it wait till September?'

Holding my hand, Bekah said, 'Mr Sharma, could you explain to my husband why waiting until September is not a good idea?'

They all knew that time was of the essence. We needed to catch this thing before it went any further. There was no time to lose.

I was booked in within a fortnight.

4

Fixing the faucet

The verb 'to nag' is defined by Oxford Learner's Dictionaries as: 'To keep complaining to somebody about their behaviour or keep asking them to do something.'[1] That 'something' may be trivial and mundane, such as cutting the lawn, taking out the bins or doing some long-overdue DIY. Sometimes it's more serious than that, like going to the dentist today rather than leaving it until tomorrow. Whatever the 'something' is, the word denotes a degree of discomfort for the one on the receiving end. Perhaps that's why, when used as an adjective, it is applied to pain, as in 'a nagging injury'. To be nagged is to be irritated.

Nowhere is the word 'nag' used more frequently than in the context of marriage. At the risk of sounding sexist, I think it's fair to say that in the world of traditional comedy, especially stand-up comedy, the word has often been used in relation to wives.

Here's a well-known example.

---

[1] 'Nag', Oxford Learner's Dictionaries: https://www.oxfordlearnersdictionaries.com/definition/english/nag (accessed 7 November 2023).

A husband, oppressed by his ever-nagging wife, decides to take her on holiday to Jerusalem. He hopes the gesture will help to cheer her up and soften her attitude.

Halfway through their stay, the wife unexpectedly dies.

The widower goes to see a funeral director.

'You have two choices,' the director says in a grave tone. 'You can either pay £45,000 to have her shipped home, or £500 to bury her here in Jerusalem.'

Without hesitation, the husband says, 'Ship her home.'

The funeral director is amazed. 'Sir, why didn't you take the cheaper option?'

The husband answers, 'Because a long time ago a man was buried in this very city, and three days later he rose from the dead. I simply can't take the chance…'[2]

The Merriam-Webster dictionary definition of the verb 'to nag' is 'to irritate by constant scolding or urging'.[3] The husband in the Jerusalem joke would relate to that. Although it can be applied more broadly – for example, a daughter complaining about her mother nagging her to clean her room – it is most often used about wives who badger their husbands.

One of the most famous figures of the Bible's Old Testament is King Solomon. He is associated with extraordinary levels of heavenly wisdom. I'm not sure how accurate that picture is, given the evidence. First, it is said that he had 700 wives. Which also means 700 mothers-in-law. Pointing this out places me at risk of being accused of another kind of gender stereotyping, so I'll leave it at that.

Anyway, Solomon had this to say in the book of Proverbs (Proverbs are basically tweet-length aphorisms):

---

[2] Adapted from M. Stibbe and J John (compiled), *A Box of Delights* (Oxford: Monarch Books, 2001).

[3] 'Nag', Merriam-Webster: https://www.merriam-webster.com/dictionary/nag (accessed 1 November 2023).

'A nagging spouse is like the drip, drip, drip of a leaky faucet; you can't turn it off, and you can't get away from it.'

(Proverbs 27:15-16, MSG)

If this man really did have 700 wives, the law of probabilities suggests that these rather melancholy words reflected his experience of at least one of them.

Why is this important?

I think it's because we often mistake constant questioning born from genuine concern (a positive quality) for pestering (a negative one). There are occasions when a loved one knows or suspects there is something that needs immediate and urgent attention, and that this something is far more important than the garden fence or a dripping tap. It's something to do with our health. It's something that could be sinister if not looked at straightaway. When they apply pressure to make sure we get it checked out, that's not a vice; it's a virtue. We may think it's intrusive, but it's not.

I founded and run a magazine called *Sorted*, voted the world's most wholesome men's magazine, so you could say that I'm very passionate about inspiring men. I know from experience that men generally respond badly to nagging. Maybe we could do ourselves a favour and get better at it.

You may wonder why I've spent this long talking about nagging. Maybe you're even beginning to feel a little badgered, even nagged, by me. The reason I'm mentioning it is that this whole journey I'm on started with my wife expressing her concern about something she saw on the underside of my foot.

I was lying on the bed, my feet sticking out, as Bekah was coming out of the ensuite in our bedroom one day. She looked at my right foot hanging over the end of our bed.

'What's that?'

'What's what?'

'There's a little dark spot, like a blood blister.'

'Oh, it's just me overwalking the dog.'

'I'm not sure. I think you should get that looked at.'

After that, she kept asking if I'd done what she'd suggested. I pointed out that we were in the middle of a lockdown. No one was *speaking with*, let alone *seeing*, a doctor.

As it happened, the lockdown was a blessing in disguise for me. Like most men, I hate going to the doctor or to hospital. Covid made this practically impossible. However, I realised I could take a photo of the black spot and email it to the surgery. I thought this would lead to a reassuring diagnosis and some cream.

It did not.

My doctor referred me to a dermatologist in nearby Worthing, so off I went to see him. We got on like a house on fire. In fact, I even showed him a magic trick while he was examining me. He was impressed.

'I'm going to ask you to come back in a fortnight or so,' he said, 'so I can do a biopsy.'

I wasn't too keen on waiting. It was his turn to show off his skills. It was only fair.

'Why can't you do it now, Doc?'

He paused, then nodded. 'All right.'

He performed the procedure.

Two weeks later, I was at home watching... Yes, you guessed right. It was a Thursday afternoon, and I was drinking a big mug of coffee in front of *The Chase*. My phone went and it was my new BFF, the dermatologist, informing me I had skin cancer.

Why am I telling you this?

I love my wife dearly (strange name, I know), but in my mind she had become the proverbial nag – less of a dripping tap and more of a police water cannon. She'd spotted a tiny mark, one that hadn't been there before, and something that couldn't be removed with a good scrub. She asked me to get it checked out, but because it didn't hurt, I left it. Unimpressed by my masculine nonchalance, she kept on at me. Eventually, I agreed.

I'm very glad I did.

I'm on a journey that I didn't expect to be on, but I've learned a valuable lesson. Nagging from someone who loves you is an act of love, not antagonism. Bekah may be outstandingly stubborn, but she was also outstandingly committed to performing acts of heroic dedication – driving me to hospital appointments, freezing in car parks all day while she waited, bringing me breakfast in bed so I could take painkillers before I got up, getting up at 6 a.m. to walk the dog because I couldn't, changing grotty dressings when I couldn't shower for six weeks. She's a legend.

And here's the point: she only nagged because I ignored her. Nagging wouldn't exist if we responded more quickly to genuine worries, so maybe we need to recognise that there'd be no drip, drip, dripping if we got up and fixed the leaky tap. Once I'd seen the medical expert, I at least knew what was wrong. And then the dripping stopped.

I'm so conscious of how many of us, especially blokes, just don't like being told to do, even though we know deep down in our hearts what we need to do. We don't realise that the pressure being applied to us is generated by love and concern.

I, for one, am glad that I fixed the tap and the dripping stopped. You may be surprised at that. *Wouldn't you have preferred to live with the nagging and just not known?* No, I wouldn't. The truth is, knowing what we're facing has brought me and Bekah so much closer. We appreciate each other more. We're more grateful for each other. Fixing the tap has ultimately been a good thing.

Earlier this year, Bekah wrote these words on her Facebook page. It was our anniversary. She called it 'Fifteen Years':

15 years married to my darling.

15 years of laughing at his jokes, his quirks and anything else that makes us lose ourselves in belly laughs.

15 years of holding hands on walks, nestling under his chin and snuggling on a sofa.

15 years of crazy family, blood and beyond; of
    of friendships, fun and adventure.
15 years of challenges, hardships and tears.
15 years of following Jesus, trusting him in the
    challenges and hardships, and joining him in the adventure
    he's set before us.
15 years in sickness and in health, on holiday and in
    hospital, on sunny days and drenched (to my pants) by the
    rainy days.
15 journeys around the sun, through all the seasons,
    and I'm grateful for every single day of it.

That's stunningly beautiful and deeply moving – I told you she
was amazing, right?

But it's true. We appreciate each other so much more now.

Fixing the tap has caused us to get busy living, to appreciate
every passing second we have with each other, to squeeze every
drop of goodness out of every day together.

And rather than resenting being nagged by the wife, maybe
this is what it really means to be a man. As the poet Rudyard
Kipling wrote, at the end of his poem 'If':

If you can fill the unforgiving minute
    With sixty seconds' worth of distance run –
Yours is the Earth and everything that's in it,
    And – which is more – you'll be a Man, my son.[4]

---

[4] R. Kipling, 'If' (public domain).

5

Attending to my sole

As my eyes slowly began to open, I saw a bright light. I heard someone say, 'Stephen! Stephen!' No one ever calls me Stephen except my mum. But it clearly wasn't her – the lack of chintz wallpaper gave that away. Had I died under anaesthetic and woken up in heaven? Was I being addressed formally by some heavenly official, in preparation for being processed?

As it turned out, the bright light was not an otherworldly phenomenon, and the voice was neither that of my old ma nor a celestial being. The brightness came from a hospital light, and the voice belonged to a nurse who was helping me come round.

This happened during Day Two of my treatment organised by Mr Sharma. On Day One I had been given another scan in the nuclear medicine department of a private hospital in Maidstone.

Yes, I said *nuclear*.

I was asked to lie down on a treatment couch and then given small injections of a blue radioactive liquid into the foot with the melanoma. About fifteen minutes later they conducted the scan – one designed to pick up the radioactive liquid and trace it as it moved through the lymphatic vessels and into the lymph nodes. The first nodes the tracer drained into were the sentinel nodes. The radiographer marked where these nodes were on my skin.

On Day Two, it was time for the surgery. In a strange way, I'd been impatient to get past it so we could get on with life. I don't think I felt scared; it was more like going to the wedding of a distant relative. I just wanted it over, so in a way I was sort of looking forward to it.

Bekah, however, was more apprehensive. She was thinking about the implications. As well as being concerned about my recovery and what they might find, there was the fact that we were in another lockdown and she would need to be chief carer, primary communicator with the outside world, housekeeper, nurse, dog walker, and mum, all the while trying to run Restored, a domestic abuse charity.

She didn't say all that to me, of course. She was still thinking about that night when she had slept soundly after the initial diagnosis. She remembered what I'd said about watching her sleep – that it had reassured me. I didn't know this, but that had become her guiding principle. She had to be okay, so that everyone else – me, most of all – would be okay.

We had been asked to come in early that morning, having self-isolated for a week to make sure we didn't take Covid in with us. Bekah wasn't allowed to be with me this time, so she planned a series of coffee shop visits with free car parks where she could work while I was receiving my treatment. I hoped to be out and away by early afternoon. As it turned out, she ended up sitting in the car wrapped in a blanket as she waited until almost 5 p.m. for me to be discharged.

As for the surgery itself, the surgeon made an incision on the sole of my right foot and removed an extended area of healthy skin and tissue from around where the melanoma was, to help reduce the risk of it returning. The surgical team went 2cm either side of the initial scar and 2cm deep. They also removed a sentinel lymph node from my right groin. Thank goodness this was all done under general anaesthetic.

While I was still asleep, the surgeon injected a blue dye into the area around the site of the melanoma. The dye gradually drained into the sentinel lymph nodes. Mr Sharma used a handheld scanner to pick up the radioactivity. He made a cut into my skin over the area before proceeding to remove the sentinel node. He sent this to the laboratory to see if it contained cancer cells.

It was some time after this that I woke to see that strange bright light and to hear the voice calling my name.

Once I had eaten something and been to the toilet, I was allowed to go home. This was when I realised the enormity of the challenge ahead. I wasn't allowed to use my foot at all. I couldn't apply any weight to it, so that meant crutches. But I had neither the coordination nor the strength required, so I was wheelchaired out to my wife.

Even getting into the car was a major effort. I went home with a sore foot, some new lines on my body (courtesy of the radiographer), and the sight of weird blue urine for a few days – something that gave me quite a shock the first time I visited the bathroom, and caused the family a great deal of intrigue. They suddenly knew what it would be like to live with a Smurf for a few days.

Despite having worked in her car 'office' all day, Bekah made me my favourite comfort food again that night – shepherd's pie. This was becoming a very tasty new tradition. But I was completely immobilised. I had to keep my foot elevated and could only walk to get to the toilet, into bed, or back onto the sofa. This was just as well, as I'd have killed myself – or someone else – trying to get any further on my crutches.

Even getting into bed proved to be a problem. When the time came, Bekah demonstrated how to get up the stairs by sitting on my bottom and shuffling. That sounds straightforward enough, but getting my tall frame upright at the top proved an issue, despite her having borrowed a spare set of crutches for upstairs from a friend. By the time I finally made it into bed, I was exhausted.

I was also bleeding.

Profusely.

The effort of getting upstairs, or just being upright, or maybe a combination of the two, had upset the wound. Bekah had to hold my leg up and exert serious pressure on it for what seemed like hours, though it was probably just ten minutes in reality, to stem the bleeding. It was a real mess. After that, I was terrified of knocking it in the night and restarting a major bloodbath.

All this meant that our bed sheets looked a little like the scene from *Die Hard* when John McClane had to walk on broken glass. Bekah draped everything in dark towels and found a couple of pillows to keep my foot raised.

I did my best to sleep, but I'm not sure she slept a wink. She was more worried about knocking me than I was about knocking myself.

After that first night, we realised getting upstairs wasn't going to work, so Bekah made up the sofa bed downstairs to keep the distances between the toilet, the bed and the sofa as short as possible. It was much more practical, and to me it felt a bit like glamping. I even got through a few boxsets on Netflix. But the situation left Bekah feeling lonely.

She had made me promise to call if I needed anything, and here's the thing.

I couldn't do *anything*.

I could barely use my crutches, let alone carry a glass of water. I couldn't reach down to put on my socks. I couldn't wash myself properly. I was helpless. Being bed-bathed by your wife sounds more exciting than it really is. Thoughts of intimacy were drowned in the practicalities of recovery and dependency.

I had to cancel all my gigs again, this time from January all the way to the end of March. I did manage to keep doing my day job for *Sorted*. I was the editor, but also did most of the administration, including addressing envelopes and dropping them into the postbox. It's all glamour at the top! We found a great office lap tray so I could work from the sofa.

After a few days of me calling Bekah every five minutes to bring me some stationery or a cuppa, she developed a system. She set me up each morning with a drink, a stack of envelopes and my laptop. Then she did the post run for me at the end of the day.

There were a few occasions when she needed to go away for the weekend. Two of our girls, Meggie and Maddie, were amazing dad-sitters and came home to care for me – though Meggie, our youngest, was a pretty hard taskmaster, who thought her mum had been mollycoddling me. She was way more hardcore than either Maddie or Bekah.

Even the days when Bekah had to actually go in to the office required a full-on rota of volunteers to drop in and walk the dog, bring me my lunch from the fridge, and generally check I was okay. Those people were legends. We have never ceased to be overwhelmed with gratitude for those who showed up with a cake or a lime jelly, a few beers and a pork pie, some prayer or a funny story, just to keep me company. My ability to get busy living was only possible because so many people rallied around us to help.

After two weeks, the doctor said I could finally put some weight on my heel. It felt like freedom. I was able to start doing a little more, even if I still had to engage in foot elevation ninety-five per cent of the day. It also meant I could sleep upstairs again. Never have I enjoyed my own bed so much.

The doctor was really pleased with how my foot was healing. 'Plumping out' was his phrase for it, as if he were talking about a Travelodge pillow. He even took regular photos to show his students and for me to show Bekah.

Those first photos were quite something. 'It looks like a gunshot wound,' one of the nurses declared. And it did. Although I'm not sure how that would ever happen. I can't imagine a crazed gunman ever shouting, 'Put your feet up!'

Those photos have become a source of great wonder to many of our friends, while others turn pale at the very thought of them. One of our closest friends, Tarn, has two sons, Mack and Charlie, who have enjoyed viewing every photo. I think I may have gained some serious kudos with them.

Little by little, I was recovering.

Six weeks later, I returned for a skin graft. Once again, I was put under general anaesthetic. This time, the surgeon took a thin rectangular sheet of skin from my thigh and placed it over the area where the melanoma had been. This time, there were no bright lights or strange voices when I woke up. But I was hungry.

One of the nurses asked me what I wanted for lunch. Determined to get my money's worth, I replied, 'I'll have a couple of rounds of egg mayonnaise sandwiches on brown please.'

This newly covered wound turned out to be even more fragile than the last, and Bekah gave me a stern telling off when she caught me trying to walk on my heel. It was back to sleeping downstairs and doing nothing more exciting in the day than going for a wee.

Just under a week later, I met with Mr Sharma to hear the results. Still in lockdown, Bekah wasn't allowed to come with me, so once again she waited in the carpark.

He didn't exactly look overjoyed when I entered the room. 'The wound's healing well, but I'm afraid we've found melanoma in the lymph node biopsies,' he said.

The cancer had spread.

This was not the news I wanted to hear.

6

Colbie and me

If diamonds are a girl's best friend, I've discovered that a dog is most definitely a man's best friend. That's why I want to press the pause button here and spend a few moments paying tribute to the canine companion who has helped me get busy living.

As a child, I was never allowed a dog. There was a cat who visited our house every day, but that wasn't the same. I was given a hamster I named Jinx, but Jinx wasn't a dog. He was hopeless at fetching sticks. In my heart, it was a dog I wanted.

All that changed eleven years ago. My five daughters and I had longed for a dog for a while. It was just a case of convincing my wife, who wasn't so keen. But her resistance was starting to wane.

She overheard me speaking to Meggie one day.

'Mum's weakening,' I revealed.

Meggie beamed from ear to ear.

That revelation kickstarted our search.

Then, one cold, crisp January morning, we drove to a farm near Glastonbury and picked up the last female of a large litter. If you looked at her now, you'd think she was a very svelte black

Labrador, but she's actually a mix of Labrador Retriever and Border Collie. She's technically called a Borador, but I think Labradollie works much better. Anyway, we drove home with a new family member that day.

I wanted to call her 'Jet' because of her colour (and also because Jet was my favourite Gladiator back in the day). But I was outvoted by the six women in my life when they found out about my secret Gladiator crush. The dog was as black as coal, so they decided on the perfect name.

Colbie.

Ever the big softie, I spent the first two nights sleeping next to her cage in the living room. She positioned her tiny body so it was pushed as close to mine as possible against the sides of the cage. We were destined to be best pals forever.

Since we first welcomed her into our family, Colbie has been outgoing and friendly. With the lovely, gentle temperament of a Labrador and the intelligence of a Border Collie, she was very quick to learn. We knew having a well-trained dog was important, so within weeks of our new houseguest arriving she was enrolled in puppy classes, followed by tricks, agility and flyball. We even looked into giving her search-and-rescue classes, but ironically we couldn't find any. Colbie was trained within an inch of her life and has more qualifications than I do. She can even skateboard.

That's not to say she has always been perfectly behaved. Remember how I said she was clever? Well, intelligence can be used for mischief too, as any dog owner knows.

One time, I left a cheesecake out on the worktop in the kitchen. When I returned from a visit to the post office, I noticed the whole thing had just upped and disappeared. When I called the dog through, she sat and looked at me with the guiltiest face you've ever seen. Her ears were pinned back, her eyes crying out, 'Come on, I'm much more of a Pedigree Chum kinda gal.'

But I wasn't falling for it. I never did get to the bottom of the Great Cheesecake Mystery, although I did spy something on the bridge of Colbie's long black snout. Crumbs!

Another time, during a cheese-and-wine soirée at our place (could this anecdote get any more middle class?), we served everything up in the kitchen but were all sitting out in the conservatory (clearly it could). Left alone to roam the kitchen, Colbie suddenly appeared among us with a great big chunk of cheddar in her mouth. The dog had form.

When I was ordered to take a complete rest, that included rest from dog walking. Colbie looked puzzled when I returned home from my operations. I suspect I smelled like I'd been in hospital, so that would have been strange. And she couldn't understand why she wasn't allowed to lick the area where I had received my surgery. She also tried to rest her paw where I'd had the skin graft on my thigh.

But that wasn't the thing I remember most vividly. There was something much stranger than that. I was hobbling for months during my post-op recovery, frustrated that I couldn't take Colbie out for a walk. She seemed to be feeling something deeply too, because she developed a bad limp of her own. We were close to taking her to the vet when we discovered something very odd. She only limped when she was around me. When anyone else took her out, she would walk and run like her usual self. Then when she came home, the limp would return.

This just goes to show that dogs have an extraordinary bond with their owners. Anyone who has a dog knows this. If you yawn, they will often yawn too. This is known as empathetic yawning. It highlights the depth of connection between dog and owner. But whoever heard of empathetic limping?

Colbie has been such a joy to me over the last eleven years as we've walked almost every day on the beach in L.A. Now, I know at this point you're probably thinking, *Wow, this bloke Steve leads such a glamorous life. Here he is walking his dog beside the booming waves of a Californian beach.* I don't want to burst your bubble, but I'm afraid it's not quite as exotic as it sounds.

A famous local resident once shortened the name of the place where I live – Littlehampton in West Sussex – to L.A. That resident was the legendary comedian Ronnie Barker, who owned a holiday home in the town. He used the gag in a sketch with his comedy partner, Ronnie Corbett. Barker tells Corbett he's just come back from L.A., and Corbett asks if he's referring to Los Angeles. His friend says no. He's talking about Little 'Ampton. It's been known as L.A. ever since.

You may be thinking that it would be far better to walk Colbie on a beach in California, but I'm not convinced.

Let me tell you why.

Ours is a mile-long sand-and-shingle beach that stretches out in front of everything you would expect from an established seaside resort. There's a promenade, amusements centre, theme park and even the UK's longest bench. Yes, I said *bench*! There is a 1,000-foot-long bench running along Littlehampton's seafront. What a claim to fame! To the west is Bognor Regis. Carry on walking to the east and you'll end up in Brighton, having passed Worthing on the way. It's a truly beautiful place to live, and I feel very blessed. As the Bible puts it, 'the boundary lines have fallen for [us] in pleasant places' (Psalms 16:5-8).

Most days, come rain or shine, you'll find Colbie and me walking on the beach. She loves low tide, when she can sprint along the wet sand after her ball and then charge into the sea on hot days. It's sheer bliss, and it's always been our daily routine.

A dog truly is a man's best friend. Whenever I'm away on the road, Colbie sits in my favourite chair. Whenever I'm back, she cannot wait to head to the beach. Walking my dog by the sea is a foretaste of heaven for me.

This reminds me of a heartbreaking incident in the life of children's author Roald Dahl. Dahl was a man with a shadowy side, but he was also someone who experienced extreme trauma. After his seven-year-old daughter Olivia died, he went to see Geoffrey Fisher, a former schoolteacher of his, who was

Archbishop of Canterbury at the time.

The cleric reportedly tried to help Dahl get back on his feet by encouraging him to remember Olivia's happiest moments. This backfired spectacularly, however, when Dahl suggested that the high points for his beloved daughter were the times when she had run with the family's dogs. The archbishop couldn't help but state what he believed to be true: that there would be no canine companions in heaven. It was at this point that Dahl reportedly broke down.[5]

When I think of heaven, I can't imagine it without my dog. If heaven is meant to be the perfection of all earthly experiences, then it would be imperfect if I found myself somewhere where there wasn't a long beach, the sound of the surf, and a dog walking by my side as my perfectly healed feet paddle in the warm water at the edge of the golden sand. My days with Colbie have taught me that.

Earlier in this chapter I said we are best pals forever.

I meant it when I said *forever*.

5 E. Retter, 'Inside Roald Dahl's darkest hours after tragic death of daughter laid bare on film', *The Mirror*, 18 February 2021: https://www.mirror.co.uk/news/uk-news/inside-roald-dahls-darkest-hours-23525140 (accessed 7 November 2023).

7

A case of friendly fire

'I'm going to refer you to my colleague, who's an oncology consultant,' Mr Sharma said. 'Her name is Sally. She'll start you on a course of immunotherapy as a matter of urgency.'

Mr Sharma was speaking to Bekah as well as to me. When I realised the news wasn't that good, I had asked if she could be there too. She's the brains of our outfit, and is like a medical encyclopaedia. She gets it from her mum. Every doctor, consultant and professor we've seen has assumed she's medically trained. She asked lots of great questions about what everything meant and what would come next.

'The good news is, your foot is healing well,' Mr Sharma said. 'I've had other patients try to walk too far too soon. They lost the graft altogether and we had to start again.'

He was clearly impressed at how literally I had taken the instruction to do nothing. But then I wasn't walking (or not walking, so to speak) this road alone. Bekah was running the house, walking the dog and chauffeuring me to hospital appointments, and we had great friends who stepped in when she was away. This made things a whole lot easier.

Mr Sharma was pleased. However, I was duly warned to continue the good behaviour now that he was handing me over to Sally. He explained that his area of expertise was foot reconstruction. He needed her skills for the next phase.

On 16 March 2022, we visited Dr Sally Wilson for the first time. Sally is extremely kind and compassionate. She explained everything about the treatment, recognising Bekah's need to understand every last detail, as well as my need to be positive and joke about it all. She was wonderful, except in one respect – she was always late. This is something that makes me very stressed. When Bekah talks about this character trait of mine, she is adamant that I'm on the spectrum. She may or may not be right, but I like things to happen to plan and on time. I get very cranky if people rock up two hours late.

As we checked in at reception, the woman behind the desk smiled at us. 'She's running late.' Then she added, 'She usually does.'

My nerves were jangling before I even sat down.

Fortunately, Covid restrictions were easing, so Bekah was allowed into the meeting. She held my hand, smiled in her slightly amused-at-me way and said, 'We have all day. It doesn't matter.'

But it did to me.

Bekah has since pointed out that the reason Dr Wilson is always late is because she's so good at her job and takes the time to ensure that her patients are okay before they leave. However, the rigid medical system doesn't allow for that kind of personal, relational input.

It still winds me up, though!

At last, we got to see her.

It turned out she was wonderful, and we clicked so quickly that we were on first name terms straight away. Sally explained how immunotherapy worked: 'It's like sending your immune system to school. The first dose is like nursery. The second, infant school. Then on and on until it has a master's degree in recognising the enemy [melanoma] and killing it.'

That was clear enough.

'Chemotherapy and radiotherapy don't really work with melanoma,' she said, 'but over the years, doctors have started to realise that the immune system eventually starts to recognise and react to melanoma. It's just that usually it does that far too late. Immunotherapy is meant to boost the system and speed up the process.'

Then came the less positive news.

'The downside is this: your immune system can become a bit trigger-happy and identify the wrong thing as the enemy, then target and attack it. For example, this friendly fire might kill off your thyroid gland or your kidney, or attack your gut. If that happens, you need to stop immunotherapy and have remedial treatment for the damage done to the mistaken target.'

If the educational analogy had been clear and comforting, this military picture was more sobering.

Nevertheless, we decided it was worth the risk.On Wednesday 6 April 2022, I arrived at the Sussex Cancer Centre in Brighton and began the first round of immunotherapy. In my case, a powerful drug called pembrolizumab was used. This helps your immune system to kill cancer cells. It's an effective treatment for various specific types of cancer.

It was administered every six weeks via a drip into my bloodstream on the chemotherapy ward. It wasn't painful, but I was told to look out for side effects. I was given a long list of possible symptoms to study and told to look out for them.

I didn't experience any of them. The only thing I did feel was hot and uncomfortable on the ward. I distracted myself by watching comedy shows on my iPad.

Although the doctors had said the treatment would only last thirty minutes, I had resigned myself to the probability that I would be there all day. I was right.

As this process continued, Bekah noticed something. She had been changing the dressings and cleaning the wound on my foot as it healed. One day, I saw her looking puzzled. She started prodding around the edge of the wound.

'I think you've got more melanoma growing,' she said. 'Right here, outside the wound.' She looked back through some of the older photos and realised this new black mark had been there for a while, hidden among the scabs and scar tissue. This gave us a fright and made us realise we weren't out of the woods yet.

Off we went back to Mr Sharma, who promptly cut it out.

'This does happen, and it isn't the end of the world,' he added in a calm, reassuring voice. 'Hopefully, immunotherapy will stop more of these recurring in the future.'

This wasn't the only challenge I faced. Sitting on the sofa for three months had taken its toll on my muscles. Bekah had been nagging at me to do some exercises to stop muscle wastage, but I still hadn't really learned my lesson about listening to her.

Getting back on my feet wasn't easy. Walking around the house was manageable; I just used my heel for weeks. But when I was finally allowed out, it was a whole different story.

The day came when I was well enough to leave the house and visit our favourite cafe on the beach. Bekah took me inside, then left to walk the dog. I sat and watched the waves.

Just getting from the car to the cafe – a mere twenty metres – was exhausting. I didn't really know how to use my whole foot any more. I was limping like a war veteran who'd lost a limb in a mine explosion.

As I started to walk a little further each day, Bekah became a drill sergeant, encouraging me to try to walk normally. Between you and me, I preferred it when she wasn't there. But then I started to develop a sore knee from the unusual gait I adopted in her absence. I decided it would be best if I paid attention to her and to others.

A friend of ours who is a physiotherapist explained that walking in sand would be good for me: 'It makes you use your whole foot in a gentle way. Just try it. You can't go on walking on your heel, no matter how stubborn you are about trying to prove your wife wrong.'

From then on, walking the dog on the beach brought with it a whole new level of health benefits. There was the fresh air, the wind in my face, the sand under my feet. It worked.

Two weeks into this phase of learning how to walk again came the first gig in my diary: Spring Harvest, a wonderful annual Christian festival held at Butlins in Minehead. In its heyday, more than 75,000 people would attend over the Easter period. I'd been working at the event every year for nearly forty years – initially stewarding, then appearing alongside one of my best pals, Ishmael, for years, helping to lead the 8-11s work with nearly a thousand children each week.

I've hosted late-night shows at Spring Harvest and sold magazine subscriptions for *Sorted* in the marketplace. For the last fifteen years, Bekah and I have been leading the all-age celebrations. I reckon over all those years put together, I've spent about eighteen months of my life in a Butlins chalet.

Those of you familiar with the event will nod knowingly when I say that I can't be sure that I have ever actually seen the sun at this gathering. Spring Harvest wouldn't be Spring Harvest without the relentless rain and gales that regularly threaten to bring down the Big Top. Perfect weather for ducks, but your Bible does tend to get wet.

Getting back there provided a great goal and incentive for my recovery.

Bekah was adamant: 'I'll take you around on piggyback if I have to!'

As it turned out, that wasn't necessary, but I did have to sit on a chair while she carried boxes and set up my *Sorted* stand. Spring

Harvest offered me a buggy, but I managed to get around on my feet, occasionally realising I wasn't as strong as I'd thought, and struggling with the restrictions caused by my lack of fitness and strength.

We had a fabulous time, though. We met lots of friends, old and new, on the *Sorted* stand, and the all-age celebrations involved bucketloads of singing, talks, fun and our nightly pantomime, 'The Good, the Bad and the Granny'. Yes, it was as daft as it sounds.

Our team, as ever, was sensational, and it was so good to be helping families spend time with God together. Late-night drinks in the Yacht Club with team members and friends made it a very special, albeit exhausting, week away. It was just what I needed. It was great to be back.

Other festivals followed that spring and summer: the Big Church Day Out, New Wine and my absolute favourite, The Gathering – around 2,500 men in a field in Swindon for a weekend. We're talking comedy, cool cars, a bar, live music, sports, inflatables, axe throwing and bonfires, alongside great worship and fantastic speakers. Imagine a cross between *Top Gear* and *Songs of Praise* and you'll get the idea. It's as crazy as it sounds, but it's a unique space where men encounter God in a way that I just haven't seen in other places. As usual, I did the thirty-minute warm-up before each session, and loved it. There's nothing like The Gathering, and it is always the festival highlight of my year.

Most Fridays and Saturdays I was on the road gigging. I did comedy nights, family events, Alpha launches, special guest services and men's breakfasts – only interrupted by the regular blood tests, scans, immunotherapy and oncology appointments. It was so good to be living (fairly) normally again.

It turned out things were not so great on the treatment front, however. I continued to get the tiny black marks on my foot, which kept being cut out and revealed as more melanoma. We feared it meant the immunotherapy wasn't working.

We were right, and in August the doctors decided to stop my treatment. It was a blow, as it meant waiting to see when it would rear its ugly head again, but on the positive side, with all the chunks cut out of my foot, I was cancer-free for a while and we were determined to enjoy the respite.

In September we went to Dorset on holiday with some friends. It was lots of fun, but I was constantly thirsty and peeing ten times a night. My eyes had become very blurry and I felt exhausted all the time. On our return home I booked an appointment at Specsavers and, more importantly, phoned my cancer nurse and told her about my symptoms.

'I want you to come to the EACU [the Emergency Ambulatory Care Unit] in Brighton as a matter of urgency,' she said. 'Be here first thing in the morning.'

After a day of tests, I was diagnosed with type 1 diabetes. *Now this on top of everything else?* I asked myself, but at least it wasn't anything more sinister going awry in my brain. We were honestly relieved.

Bekah texted this to the girls:

Hey girls. Just wanted to give you a bit of a medical update in Dad's ongoing sagas. We're in hospital at the moment, where he's being treated for high blood sugar - it looks like he's become diabetic. It explains some funny symptoms he's had over the last week or so, and it's good that he's being sorted out. It's annoying, but not a big fat worry. Love you xx

We had been warned that pembrolizumab sometimes attacked the wrong targets in the body, and that's what had happened to me. Instead of just destroying the bad stuff, it was damaging some of the good stuff, and it had destroyed my pancreas. I was a victim of friendly fire.

I went home with needles and insulin. Something else to get used to.

8

A roller-coaster ride

By Christmas 2022, we had been through every emotion imaginable. We had experienced a calm phase in the months leading up to it, and enjoyed a wonderful autumn and the beginnings of winter in L.A. (West Sussex version). A week before Christmas, that all changed.

'I'm afraid the cancer's spread,' Sally, my oncologist, said. 'It's in your groin. I don't think there's anything else we can do.' She paused before adding, 'I'm going to contact the Marsden to see if they've got any trials. I don't think they'll want you, though. You've got the wrong type of melanoma. The rare type.'

I later learned that the Royal Marsden first opened its doors in 1851 as the world's first hospital dedicated to cancer diagnosis, treatment, research and education. These days it's ranked among the top-five cancer centres in the world, treating nearly 60,000 NHS and private patients every year. It is a centre of excellence, with an international reputation for groundbreaking research as well as for pioneering the very latest in cancer treatment. I was very grateful even for the suggestion of me being treated there.

Bekah went through the whole holiday thinking, 'This is our last Christmas together.' But in true Bekah style, she kept her thoughts to herself, wanting the rest of us to just enjoy everything. She still remembered that night when her peaceful sleep had been so reassuring to me. I know now that she shared her fears and her tears with her mum, and set up a WhatsApp group with her most trusted friends, so she had a place where she could say the things she didn't want me or the girls to hear.

Days later, everything changed again. After Christmas, the Royal Marsden rang. 'You can't have the trial, but we do think it's worth operating. This could be curative.'

The word 'curative' caught our attention. Yes, I'd have to endure a major operation in January, but that would be a small price to pay if the operation worked.

Five days before my operation, it was time to celebrate my birthday. On 6 January 2023 we visited Thai Street Food, along the road in Worthing. I'd become friends with the restaurant proprietor, Yamin, and she had been keenly following my health updates on Facebook. She got very emotional when she saw me. We'd popped in for supper just before Christmas, and she'd burst into tears then, too. She listened to my updates and insisted on treating us to a meal on the house.

I told Yamin about my surgery when we returned a fortnight later, and she gave me a small golden Buddha pendant. 'They're symbols of good luck, peace and longevity,' she said. 'This will attract good energy. It will help you fight negative energy, bring more positive energy and help you overcome troubles in life.' She added, 'I'll be praying for you.'

Yamin knows I'm a Christian. I didn't put any stock in the powers of her pendant but I was very grateful for the sentiment, and I received her kindness and generosity in the spirit in which it was given.

Five days later, I was checking in to the Royal Marsden.

My surgeon was Professor Anthony Hunt, or 'the Prof', as I

called him. He has a specialist practice in soft-tissue sarcoma and advanced melanoma. Historically, he operates on more than 200 cases of sarcoma and another 100 cases of advanced malignant melanoma, as well as other rare cutaneous malignancies, every year. These days, he only performs my kind of surgery every six months or so.

We arrived in central London at 7 a.m. on Wednesday 11 January 2023, and the Prof conducted an ilio-inguinal block dissection on me. This is a form of surgery involving the removal of most of the lymph nodes from a specific part of the body. It can be performed on the neck, armpit or groin. In my case, it was the latter. As I explained earlier, lymph nodes are part of the immune system and help to fight infection.

There are potentially twenty to thirty nodes in the groin area. The Prof planned to remove as many as he could without damaging the surrounding blood vessels and nerves. As I lay on his operating table under general anaesthetic, he removed twenty-nine during the four-hour procedure. Histology later confirmed that nineteen of them contained cancer cells.

I ended up with a very impressive fourteen-inch scar. I'd asked the Prof if he could make it jagged, so it looked like a shark attack but, unimpressed, he was adamant he would do his very neatest work. Worth a try! It would have made for some interesting conversations at the beach or around the swimming pool.

Neatly operated on and sewn up, I woke up desperate for a wee, and at the same time confused. No one had told me I'd have a catheter in place. A catheter, for those not in the know, is a tube that goes into your bladder. When you need to pass urine, it is collected in a bag via the tube. This was a strange sensation for me. Since I wasn't allowed out of bed during my recovery, the catheter stayed in place for twenty-four hours. Then came another novel experience – the time for it to be removed.

The nurse put on a fresh pair of gloves as she prepared for the procedure.

'How often have you done this before?' I asked.

'It's my first time,' she joked.

I didn't have time to react to that. While I was laughing nervously, she pulled it out. I didn't really feel anything, but I'm sure my eyes watered a little.

I didn't feel like getting out of bed until the next day. I was sore and had to be given lots of pain relief. As ever, Bekah was by my side pretty much 24/7.

An old pal of mine called Jon Grubb phoned. He'd seen a Facebook post about my operation. 'I hear you're at the Marsden.'

'That's right, pal.'

'I work just around the corner from you. Fancy a visitor, a large flat white and some Danish pastries?'

'I most certainly do.'

'I'll be straight round.'

After an hour's wait, we both realised the error of our ways. Jon didn't work next door to the Marsden in Chelsea (where I was). The Marsden he was referring to was in Sutton in Surrey.

I returned home around forty-eight hours after my surgery. Regular scans continued to be a part of my new normal. Magnetic resonance imaging (MRI) is a type of scan that uses strong magnetic fields and radio waves to produce detailed images of the inside of the body. Let me explain what happens.

You lie on a bed that's moved into the scanner – a large tube containing powerful magnets. At certain times the scanner makes loud tapping noises. This is the electric current in the scanner coils being turned on and off. It's vital to keep as still as possible. My scans, used to check my brain, usually lasted between thirty to forty-five minutes. I was often so chilled I'd nod off and catch up on my beauty sleep.

I also had PET-CT scans, which combined a computerised tomography (CT) scan and a (positron emission tomography) PET scan. These give detailed information about your cancer and can also show how well a treatment is working. The CT scan takes a series of X-rays from all around your body and puts them together to create a 3D picture. The PET scan uses a mildly radioactive drug to show up areas of your body where the cells are more active than normal.

For my PET-CT scans, I needed to stop eating four to six hours beforehand. I would then change into a hospital gown or green scrubs before receiving an injection of radioactive liquid called a radiotracer about an hour before the scan. You have this injection through a small plastic tube in your arm (a cannula). It's only a small amount of radiation, but the Geiger counter they used made some pretty dramatic noises. You have to rest and avoid moving around too much during this hour. No phones, reading or music is allowed – you just lie on a bed until they're ready for you. This allows the radiotracer to spread through your body and into your tissues.

The large PET-CT machine is shaped like a doughnut (ring, not jam). Once you're in the right position, the radiographer leaves, but can see you through a window from the control room. You can talk to each other through an intercom. The couch then slowly slides backwards and forwards through the scanner, and the machine takes pictures as you move. Being tall, my scans always take longer than most. That meant overtime for the staff. I think they liked it when I visited.

The whole process is painless. And provided you're not claustrophobic, it's not frightening either.

Everything seemed to go smoothly enough. In January, I was once again declared cancer-free. But this was just the calm before the storm.

In April, we received more news we didn't want to hear. The roller coaster was descending once again.

Strap in.

9

A winter wonderland

After my New Year surgery at the Royal Marsden, I looked like I'd been in a fight with a great white shark… and lost. The multiple procedures had scarred me in both body and mind. So when the opportunity came in March to take a skiing holiday with Bekah, I was keen to go.

It was a press trip, so it wasn't going to cost us anything, plus Bekah and I needed some time as a couple. We also longed for just a few days when we wouldn't have to think about scans, side effects or next steps. After eighteen months of hospitals, surgeries and treatments, it was time to take a breather and let the wounds heal. The journey up to this point had been relentless.

The destination for our welcome minibreak was a finely crafted chalet in the stunning alpine village of Morzine. The hotel was called Chilly Powder, and its hosts served exceptional meals. We had at least two of the ingredients we needed for a memorable holiday: the great outdoors and great food. We couldn't wait.

There were two small problems. First, I had never been skiing, and second, I was recuperating from a major op and wasn't fit to start learning. Bekah is the skier, although she's a bit unconventional. I'm sure she won't mind me saying that. While she's technically good, she's also terrified of heights – a weird combination for the slopes. This can cause her to turn down a perfectly traversable run where she can 'see too far'. She ends up trembling on the edge of the piste, unable to turn and pondering whether she should either take off her skis or wait for a St Bernard dog to come and rescue her. Up to this point, she had taken our kids on budget ski trips while I stayed home and consumed the types of food that she didn't like me eating. This time we were going together. The slopes may not have been the obvious choice for Mr and Mrs Legg, but we were excited all the same.

We arrived early in the evening after an hour-long transfer from Geneva airport to find that dinner was being served. Meals at Chilly Powder are eaten communally. Guests, who are treated as extensions of the family, gather around the fire at 7:30 p.m. and take their places together at one large dining table. We weren't sure how we felt about this before we arrived. A combination of shyness and just needing some space left us feeling a little apprehensive about sitting down with people we didn't know. As it turned out, dinnertime became one of the highlights of the trip. There were around twenty adults staying, and we met such a wonderful array of people that, on top of the mouthwatering food, our conversations were rich and varied.

What we encountered at Chilly Powder was a roaring fire, beautiful canapés and delicious wine. The team members couldn't have been more helpful. They introduced themselves by name and took a genuine interest in us. They arranged for a mobile ski company to come and measure Bekah's feet and kit her out for the next day. Everything else was stored in the garage, but her boots were kept in a warm room.

It soon became apparent that we were the only guests who had never been before, and that this was a warm and welcoming hotel to which guests often returned. Each couple we met had a different story of how they had discovered the place and why they wouldn't go anywhere else now. Many had shared their discovery with friends. For some, this came down to the wonderful childcare. Chilly Powder welcomes children as warmly as it does adults. It runs a crèche and helps older children access ski school. Bekah and I were often back at the chalet earlier than the others and saw the kids being taken out for crêpes or to play in the park before being brought home in time for tea.

The location was a key draw for everyone. Chilly Powder is a five-minute walk, even in ski boots, from the bottom of the Les Prodains Express. From there, a superfast lift whisks you up to 1800m, where the vast ski slopes of Avoriaz are located. Avoriaz is one of the best entry points to the Pistes du Soleil, and is considered the largest connected ski area in the world, with twelve resorts and more than 600km of pistes. From here, everything is accessible: beginner slopes, a World Cup downhill run, hiking trails, impeccably groomed slopes and hair-raising off-piste action (including the Swiss Wall – something Bekah didn't even begin to contemplate!). You can even ski into Switzerland.

And you can also ski back to where you're staying. There are no long uncomfortable bus rides with skis digging into your neck and boots wedged under your seat. There are no long slogs at the end of the day. You can literally ski into the garden where the hot tub awaits. No wonder people keep returning.

So how did we – a decidedly trepid couple – manage on our short skiing holiday?

Good question.

Very well, as it turned out.

We got up slowly and enjoyed a leisurely breakfast as the others were leaving to catch the first lift. We explored the town of Morzine and found more places to eat. We also took the fast lift to Avoriaz, so we could enjoy the snow.

Avoriaz proved to be a spectacular place to visit. Perched on the edge of a ravine, it cannot be accessed by car in the winter. Instead, a fleet of horse-pulled sleighs act as taxis. To get anywhere, you need to ski, take a lift or relive your childhood Christmas fantasy by taking a sleigh ride, complete with jingling bells. It's a proper winter wonderland. For us, it was just what we needed.

Across the piste from the top of Les Prodains Express was a restaurant and bar called La Tanière. There we found swathes of outdoor tables and deckchairs. These faced out over the valley of Les Prodains, with its impressive set of green, blue and red ski runs.

We crossed the piste, chose a seat, ordered a coffee and applied some sunscreen. When Bekah felt brave enough, she went off to explore, leaving me happily basking in the sunshine and reading the latest Jeffrey Archer. She was nervous to begin with (about the skiing, not the Jeffrey Archer novel), but quickly discovered the resort is cautious in its grading of slopes. She became confident that even red slopes were manageable. She stayed within the bowl of the mountain in front of her so her vertigo wouldn't be a problem.

It was warm while we were there, unseasonably so. One day, the temperature rose to nearly twenty degrees, which left Bekah wilting in her ski gear and me sitting in a T-shirt sipping a beer. I was concerned the sun would make it difficult to ski.

'What's the snow like?' I asked Bekah when she returned.

'At the bottom of the slopes, it's slushy. Down in Morzine it's more grass than snow, but there are plenty of slopes in the shade. And you can always get a lift above the freezing line.'

The next day, Bekah came back smiling after her ski session.

'How did you get on?'

'I set out to another section of the mountain and found some gentler pistes. Not scary at all. I practised my parallel turns. I toyed with carving, but mostly just enjoyed going on a really good journey and not simply repeating the same runs.'

I pretended to know what she was talking about. 'You should have stayed out longer.'

'I could have. The pistes I was on connected me with Morzine, Les Gets and Montriond, but I didn't want to go there by myself. I wanted to get back and spend time with you.'

And that was what it was all about.

Time.

Together.

There were walking trails, which in previous years we might have explored in snowshoes, taking in the mesmerising views together. The kind of trails I like – walking downhill and catching a lift back up to a welcoming bar.

But not this year.

This year it was about being gentle, enjoying each other's company and taking in the beauty the world has to offer. Chilly Powder gave us just that. We were able to relax, let other people take care of us, and explore our winter wonderland at our own pace.

It couldn't have been more perfect.

To us, it was heaven on earth.

10

Dandelion seeds

On Monday 17 April 2023, Bekah and I travelled together to Brighton to see my oncologist. The plan was to have our appointment and then drive to Gatwick Airport to pick up Gemma and Meggie, who were due to return that day on a long-haul flight from Australia. They had been on the trip of a lifetime, attending a family wedding and seeing relatives. We knew they would be full of excitement and stories, and we were so looking forward to seeing them again, but first we had to see Sally.

Sally is a quite remarkable person and always goes the extra mile for her patients. She has tremendous empathy and confidence, plus she knows what she's talking about, which puts us at our ease.

Usually when we went to see her, her eyes beamed out from behind her round glasses.

Not this time. This time, she wore her sad face. We knew the moment we opened the door that the news wasn't going to be positive. If there's a smiley face and lots of laughter when you enter, you know everything's okay. The opposite means it's time to prepare yourself.

I need to be honest and confess that I was already in a poor state of mind because we were being seen late. My hospital stress levels tend to be more about the wait than the treatment. That's why I had asked Sally to phone me in the past instead of me seeing her in person, but that just wasn't how she worked.

'I want you to come in,' she would say.

'Just *phone* me,' I'd insist. 'That way I can get on with other stuff while I'm waiting.'

'No, no. It's better face-to-face.'

'I disagree, Doc. It's pointless.'

I had adopted this view because they always used to say to me, 'We're not going to examine you.'

If they're not going to do that, why go?

Add the fact that the waiting area is so depressing. The walls are littered with posters about cancer. And the leaflets and booklets are terrible, too. They reassure you that cancers can appear in the weirdest places in your body. There's adenoid, appendix and penile cancer, to name just three of the more unusual ones. Who knew you could get cancer in those places? I didn't need to make myself more miserable reading that. I would much rather be at home, even if it was terrible news.

Let me give you an example from just a week ago. My most recent appointment was at 2:40 p.m. on a Wednesday. The hospital eventually phoned to talk to me at 4:55 p.m. If we'd driven to Brighton, we wouldn't have got home till 7 p.m. because of the rush hour.

Anyway, back to Sally. This time we were there in person.

'I need to talk through what we've found,' she said. 'The spot in your brain we were looking at is still there, and two more have appeared.' Worse was to follow. 'The PET scan revealed tumours in your liver, stomach, brain and spine.'

Medics often talk about melanoma as being like blowing a dandelion; the seeds spread far and wide.

As she heard Sally's words, Bekah thought to herself, *That's happened so fast. The scans in January showed nothing. Now the cancer has multiplied.*

'I'm afraid this really is the end of the road,' Sally said. 'We've run out of treatment options. Although we can do some things to alleviate symptoms… namely, palliative care.'

The treatments available were some radiotherapy on my brain and a last-ditch immunotherapy treatment, but from the beginning of our journey we'd thought this was pointless. We knew there was only a ten per cent chance of it working, and the side effects were horrible. I also knew that this was an old treatment that had been superseded by the newer treatment I'd received a year ago, which hadn't worked. This one was even less likely to work than the one I'd already had. It was also more likely to bring on another friendly fire situation, and I'd had quite enough of those.

I eventually bit the bullet and asked the big question: 'How long have I got, Doc? Five days? Five weeks? Five months? Five years?'

Bekah was relieved I'd asked. She wanted to know, but she was also scared to ask in case I didn't.

Sally paused.

I thought she would say, 'Fifteen years, maybe twenty.'

'More like five months,' she said.

I was speechless.

'How are you financially?' she asked.

'If Steve can't work, we'll struggle,' Bekah replied.

'Then it's time to contact your life insurance people.'

'What, *now*?' Bekah asked.

Sally explained. 'If you've got less than twelve months to live, they'll start releasing the money now. So when you get home, contact them. They'll send me the forms. I'll tick all the boxes. I'll make sure they know it's time.'

More shock waves.

'What on earth are we going to tell the girls?' I asked.

Sally shifted into practical mode. 'You go with the nurse and have some more blood tests, then both of you come back and see me before you leave. We'll talk about that then.'

And that's the reason why Dr Sally Wilson is always late. She cares about her patients. She isn't ruled by the clock or by the schedule. She is governed by what her patients need.

I went out onto the ward and the nurse took some bloods.

'Would you like a drink?' she asked afterwards.

'Oh, I'll have a large brandy after hearing that news, please. On the rocks.'

That made the nurse laugh. It made me chuckle, too.

'You probably haven't got that,' I said. 'So I'll have some water, please.'

We returned to Sally and chatted about how and what to tell the girls. We were due to pick the returning two within the hour.

As we turned to leave, we had one of those *Columbo* moments. You know what I'm talking about – those moments when Lieutenant Columbo (played by Peter Falk) turns to the suspect on his way out of the door. He always says, 'One more thing...'

'Oh, by the way, Steve,' Sally called out. 'You're not allowed to drive any more.'

All I could think of to say by way of a reply was, 'Please, Doc, if you've got any more bad news, just break it to me now.'

'No, that's it.'

Sally leaned in to hug me as she said goodbye. For some reason, I backed off, and I felt very bad about that afterwards.

'Thank you,' Bekah said, hugging Sally. 'You've been so kind to us this morning.'

Bekah says that one of Sally's greatest gifts is her empathy. She has this ability to feel what her patients feel, to know what her patients need. One time Bekah had told her, 'Steve's skin is very scaly and flaky. I've been rubbing and massaging cream into those areas, but I don't suppose it will make much difference in the scheme of things.'

Sally replied, 'There's really not much you can do for him, but if that makes you feel you're at least doing something, do it.'

That's empathy.

As we left, Sally said, 'God bless.'

Just as she always did.

11

A time for tears

'There's an opportune time to do things, a right time for everything on the earth… A right time to cry and another to laugh, a right time to lament and another to cheer,' (Ecclesiastes 3:1-4, MSG). So said King Solomon, the wisest person alive at the time. Looking back over the last two years, I think he was right.

After our appointment, we returned to the car and headed to Gatwick. I handed Bekah the keys so she could drive. I am one of those obedient people who does what I'm told when someone in authority gives me an instruction. I didn't want a prison sentence on top of everything else.

Bekah phoned to tell her mum the latest news. Daphne was lovely – kind and supportive, as ever. She offered to call Bekah's siblings with the updates.

Then we prepared ourselves for our girls.

We decided we would let Gemma and Meggie share about their time in Australia first. Bekah was determined they should not only have the joy of doing the trip, but the joy of talking about it, too. I resolved to sit in the front with my back to the girls so they wouldn't be able to see my tears. I would try my hardest to nod in the right places. I put on my sunglasses to conceal my puffy, red eyes.

That day we did something we don't normally do. We walked into the Arrivals area and waited. After the hugs, the girls started telling us their stories as we were walking back to the car.

During the journey home, Bekah and I were in two head spaces at the same time. Our minds were racing because of what we'd just heard at the hospital. We were trying to process what Sally had told us. We were also responding to the excitement of the stories we were hearing. We wanted the girls to extend their holiday for as long as they could. Neither of us wanted to burst their bubble.

When we got home, Bekah talked to Gemma and Meggie while I went upstairs to my office.

'It's much, much worse than we were expecting,' she told them. 'There's nothing more they can do except palliative care. There's not much time left.'

Gemma and Meggie came upstairs and gave me a big hug. The tears flowed, but I told them everything was going to be okay.

Bekah then texted Amber, Emmie and Maddie:

Hey girls. Dad had an appointment this morning to get the results of his latest scans. It's not very good news. They have shown some marks in more lymph nodes in his abdomen, in his brain and in his liver. They don't think it's curable, but they're going to ask the Royal Marsden again if he can join a trial. We've got to wait to hear more, but wanted to let you know.

We're cooking a big tartiflette tomorrow, so if you want to come over to be together or ask questions, just come.

And you can ask any questions first, of course.

Love you all very much.

And no one has to wait till tomorrow to come over either if you want to pop round today! xx

Everyone was living nearby at the time. We were so grateful that Emmie had moved back to town from her old job in Newmarket. That night, all our girls came for dinner – and the following two nights, too.

There were lots of hugs and tears.

While these evenings were very special, I couldn't join the others for the meal parts. I was so sad that I don't think I really ate much that week at all, although it was lovely overhearing their chatter in the kitchen. They were recollecting things from years back – usually something silly or embarrassing I'd done – so there was lots of laughter.

Bekah also told my parents. This was beyond tough. I had lost my little brother a few years earlier. Around Christmas time, David had started dragging his leg around, and it turned out he had glioblastoma, a brain cancer. He died the following September. So my parents had already been down this road. It was unthinkable that they should have to do it again.

Both in their early eighties, they're still very sprightly and active. A few years ago my dad had a stent fitted in his heart, yet within days he was back out helping his elderly neighbours, all of whom were about ten years younger than him, with their gardens. Mum is a little hard of hearing, so phone calls are difficult. For that reason, Bekah shared the necessary information in a text first – very similar to the one she had sent the girls.

Then she phoned them.

That was extremely hard.

Losing one child is a parent's worst nightmare. But potentially losing two is beyond imagination.

'We can't lose both our sons!' they cried.

After that, it was time for our friends and wider family to know. Facebook was a blessing. I posted an update about my prognosis, asking those who know us to pray:

It's not good news, I'm afraid. My most recent scans have shown some melanoma in more lymph nodes in my abdomen, spine, brain and liver. They don't think it's curable, but they are going to ask the Royal Marsden again if I can join a trial. Plus, I'll get some radiotherapy to try to blast the ones in my brain. We've got to wait to hear more, but wanted to let you know. I guess as far as the medical profession is concerned there's nothing more to be done, but my faith tells me this might not be the end, and there may be a few twists and turns to come. Pray for us, my beautiful wife Bekah and our five gorgeous daughters. We could really do with it even more now. Thanks.

The response was staggering: more than a thousand responses and comments, and nearly 200 shares. We felt massively uplifted. We heard later that churches all across the world, from Bournemouth to Buenos Aires, were praying for my healing. I felt so loved and appreciated, and that made me cry. Again.

Every new comment brought more tears. Some sad tears, but mainly tears of gratitude at the kindness of friends and strangers. It was overwhelming.

A few close pals came to visit straight away. Ishmael arrived in a flash, and has kept coming every fortnight. Our friend Sarah Smith brought me little treats and has helped Bekah change my dressings on more than one occasion. Once a nurse, always a nurse. A fellow evangelist and one of my oldest mates, Steve Lee, arrived with a bag of beers, a family-sized pork pie and lots of encouragement. He anointed me with Sainsbury's Finest olive oil, but spilled the bottle on the floor of our conservatory in the process. He's a big boy, too, and just as clumsy as me. Once we had stopped laughing, his prayers were very powerful. His visit and all the others in those first few days meant so much.

Our friend Debra Green, who heads up Redeeming our Communities (ROC), set up a JustGiving page for people to give towards what we called our 'summer of joy'.

It raised a staggering £15,000.

If all we had was five months, we were determined to get busy living while there was still time.

There had been a time for tears.

But now it was time for joy as well.

12

On the road again

After hearing the bad news on the Monday, I was aware that I had four comedy gigs coming up, starting on the Thursday and running over the course of the weekend.

Should I cancel?

Or should I go?

At first, I really didn't feel I could make, or even wanted to make, people laugh. I wasn't able to string many sentences together without my eyes welling up. I asked a good chum of mine – one of my favourite comedians and also a Christian, the brilliant Tony Vino – to be on standby. Over the next few days, I spoke with several speaker and performer mates – people like Jonathan Veira, Ishmael and Carl Beech – and they all urged me to do the shows if I possibly could. This wasn't just a job for me; I wasn't just going to be funny and make people laugh. It was my calling to tell as many people as I could, in as many places I could, the good news about Jesus. And he would be with me. They figured my latest news would add an extra string to my bow.

Sally had said to Bekah, 'Steve can work for as long as he feels well enough.'

I felt well enough, so I forced myself into the zone, put on my big boy pants and got on with it.

Bekah cancelled her entire diary. She was supposed to be away speaking that weekend. She said to herself, *We're going to do this together, and do whatever it takes to enable Steve to be who God created him to be for as long as possible.*

She drove us to the first venue. On the way, we talked about what we could do to strengthen my immune system. We often spoke with our very close GP friend, Dr Ken Ferguson, and en route took another phone call from another medic, Dr Ben, who I knew was into holistic medicine and was a melanoma survivor himself. He suggested some dietary changes, vitamins and a daily three-minute cold shower. This might not have made any difference, but in a strange way it made us feel positive because we were taking some kind of control over what we were doing. We ordered the vitamins he recommended and thought about how to eat differently, though I did wonder if the cold showers suggestion was a gag or a genuine way to increase dopamine levels. In a world where so much was out of our control, at least we were doing something.

The first gig was at my in-laws' church in Gloucester. They were planning to come with my young niece and nephews, but I asked them not to. I knew that seeing their lovely faces would set me off, so they agreed to stay away.

We arrived in plenty of time. I set up my props, then hid at the back. A few lovely people who know my in-laws found me. They came up and asked, 'How are you?'

'Do you mind if I don't talk about this now?' I replied. 'I need to concentrate on being funny.'

'I'm so sorry.'

'No, you don't have to be. Thanks for caring.'

I had to get into the zone. I didn't want to be reminded of sad thoughts.

This happened a lot, so Bekah became my gatekeeper. It was the church where she'd grown up, so she knew lots of the people. She warded them off, saying, 'Come over here and I'll talk to you.'

That night, I bounded onto the stage and did my thing. I was really pleased, and thought I'd done a good job.

'You were amazing,' Bekah said.

We stayed over, and the following day headed off to Norfolk for three more shows. As the weekend progressed, things became easier. By Sunday morning I was talking openly about the prognosis and my cancer journey so far. My friends had said my story would add something powerful, and they were right.

Of those three days, Bekah says, 'It was weirdly one of the best weekends of our marriage. We'd booked into a hotel, and we just mooched and enjoyed each other in a way that perhaps was only possible because we suddenly understood that every moment mattered. We went out for coffee. On Saturday afternoon we went to the pub, got out the laptop, and went through our diary. We started to ask some big questions: What do we want to do? What do we *not* want to do? Who do we want to see? Who do we *not* want to see?' What is important? And more critically, *who* is important? We made plans until the end of July. We didn't know what to do beyond that.'

Deciding who we wanted to spend time with was very liberating in a strange way. I'm generally Mr Nice Guy. If someone says they'd like to meet up or go out for a coffee with me, I usually say yes. But my medical situation has given me the liberty to say no.

People are lovely, but I just want to crack on with stuff and be as normal as possible. I don't want to be asked about my illness all the time. For me, this was and continues to be very important. My constant thought was: *Wouldn't it be lovely to have a couple of days where I don't even think about cancer?*

A friend of ours, Ems Hancock, gave us a very helpful pointer: 'Spend time with radiators and waterfalls. Spend time with people who radiate warmth, with whom you don't have to say very much. You feel comfortable with them. You can just snuggle up to them. They're radiators. Then there are waterfalls. Waterfalls are inspirational. They're good company, too.'

She went on to explain how this differs from the normal categories. 'Traditionally, it's waterfalls and drains. Drains drain you. Waterfalls energise you. This doesn't mean you'll never see drains. It's just that you're aware of who they are.'

We made the decision to spend most of our time with radiators and waterfalls. We only had so much time and energy.

If you're struggling with this idea, put yourself in my shoes (size 10 Hush Puppies, if you must know). If you only had 150 days left to live, who would you want to spend time with? People mean well, but sometimes they're just not helpful.

Like the guy who came up to me at a festival.

'How are you?' he asked.

'I'm good, thanks.'

'No, how *are* you?'

'I'm really good.'

'No, how are you *really?*'

'I'm great.'

'No, I mean what's the prognosis?'

'Listen, buddy, I just don't want to talk about it.'

A few days later, I was interviewed on the radio.

'How are people being with you?' I was asked.

'Really kind, but often they don't know what to say.' I related what had happened. 'One bloke asked me four times how I was, and I clearly didn't want to talk about it. That's muppetry of the highest order. Some days I just want to wake up and forget about what I'm facing. It's draining, especially if I'm at a big event and he's the hundredth person asking me that day.'

As it happened, that man was listening in. He texted me the following day and said, 'I'm sorry for being a muppet.'

That was lovely. I replied, 'No problem, Gonzo'.

We both laughed.

Some men are prepared to learn.

I deliberately say 'men', because men are particularly prone to behaving stupidly in the context of life-threatening illness.

Another time I was at a weekend for blokes. I was busy setting up my *Sorted* stand with my good buddy Andy Godfrey. Within minutes of arriving, a guy came up to me and said, 'Keep fighting, Brother.'

I said thank you.

'Yeah,' he continued. 'I lost my brother to cancer two days ago. Keep fighting, though.'

I thought, *How is this helpful?*

One mate didn't get in touch at all, then one day Bekah bumped into him at a garden centre.

He said, 'I keep meaning to message Steve, but I don't know what to say. This morning I nearly asked him how he was. But that's just such a stupid question!'

Bekah disagreed. 'No, it's a good question. It gives him the freedom to say he feels terrible because he's dying. Or, and this is far more likely, he can tell you it's an awesome morning, he's had a lovely time on the beach walking the dog and he's looking forward to having a beer with you.'

It's not just me, though. Bekah has also had to go through this. Work has sometimes provided a bit of respite, giving her something else to focus on. For the most part, her colleagues have been amazing. But one time, someone got it wrong.

Bekah recalls meeting with someone to review a document.

'How are you?' the person asked.

'I'm fine.'

That wasn't good enough. 'Bekah, I asked you how you are. It's important to be vulnerable.'

Bekah kept her thoughts to herself. *I don't want to be vulnerable right now. If I want to concentrate on this boring document, let me.*

She talked with a colleague about this afterwards, who said

something we have found very helpful: 'Other people just need to ask you what you need.'

That's such good advice. If you're with a person who's going through tough stuff – maybe it's terminal cancer, maybe it's something else – then think about what they need. If you don't know, ask them to tell you.

'Do you need me to listen to your story?'

'Do you need me to make you laugh?'

'Do you need me to take you out for a walk?'

'Do you need me to talk about my problems so you can forget about yours?'

'What do you need me to be to you right now?'

'Do you need me to pray?'

'Do you need me to do something practical?'

Be prepared to ask those questions every time you meet that person. What they need may change each day.

But we're all different. For me personally, I wanted people to help me forget about cancer. That doesn't mean I've been closed to the idea of remembering things, just so long as those things are funny or positive.

Like this, for example.

I was telling my oldest buddy, Ishmael, how one of the drugs was making me sweat profusely, especially when I was on stage. I was doing a church gig in the Midlands at that time, and I asked the hosts to have a couple of electric fans on the stage. It was a baking hot summer's day, so they weren't making a massive difference.

'I also need you to open all the windows and doors to keep me cool,' I said.

It was a fabulous event, but I still came off stage looking like manic stand-up comic Lee Evans after a set at the Wembley Arena – totally drenched in sweat.

The minister wrote to me a couple of weeks later:

Thanks so much for coming. Just to let you know, a lady was walking past the church with her son. Because the windows and doors were all open, she heard the laughter coming from inside the building. They came in for your show, and they've been coming to church since then.

That really struck me. I could have stayed home and continued crying, but I got back on the road again and kept people laughing.

And in the process, God used my problem with sweating as an opportunity to draw a mother and son into his house.

He's amazing.

13

A summer of joy

Once Bekah and I had 'done the diary', we got busy living. Sally had told us we could choose one of two things in response to my prognosis: to live dying, or to die living. I was determined to do the latter. Together with our girls, we would have a summer of joy. We would have a season of our lives enjoying some big events, but mostly choosing to find the joy in everyday things: in birdsong, sunshine and snuggles together on the sofa.

During these well-lived days, we found much joy in food. Having instituted a family dinner night, the girls took it in turns to put in their orders for old favourites: pulled pork, homemade pizza, barbecues, paella and steak nights. We got busy in the kitchen and outside on my Big Green Egg, cooking up feasts for the girls some nights and our pals on others. Some of our friends also took us out for lunch or dinner.

There came a point after about six weeks when we realised the pace had become somewhat relentless, and that we were losing time to just be, especially with our girls. We stepped back and made sure we had space to enjoy normal family time. We didn't need to be in a race to fit everyone else into our summer of joy.

Thanks to the kindness of more people than we know how to thank, we received some really special treats. As a family, we have had a long-standing love affair with *Mamma Mia!* and all things ABBA. As what is sometimes referred to as a 'new man', I'm not afraid to admit that. We booked a table for *Mamma Mia! The Party* at the O2 arena in London, something we could never normally afford to do. It was quite something. Part of the venue had been adapted to look like a beautiful taverna on the island of Skopelos, where much of the first *Mamma Mia!* movie was shot. It was like being in a Greek island paradise, sitting at rustic tables in a courtyard with a fountain, olive trees and bougainvillaea. They even cranked up the temperature, so it felt like the Med.

Using a mix of dialogue and song, the story unfolded around our tables as we enjoyed a delicious four-course Greek meal. It ended with the main floor being transformed into a 1970s disco, where everyone danced to the ABBA music. As a family, we had dressed up for the occasion and had an outstanding time eating, singing and dancing.

I say dancing, but it was the girls who did that.

I watched through tear-stained eyes.

I felt so proud of my Dancing Queens and the women they have become. I love the fun they have together. I suppose I was aware that I didn't want it all to stop. I wanted to watch them dance again and again. I wanted to watch them through all the seasons of their lives.

Bekah took hold of my hand and smiled. Her eyes were watery, too. We didn't need to say anything.

Our summer of joy had its brightest day in early June, when our first granddaughter, Marla Eve, was born. Before she arrived, I suggested she should be called 'Stevie', which was shot down in flames on more than one occasion. 'Eve', though, was a little nod to her Pops.

As I held her for the first time, the tears flowed again. I was overwhelmed by this precious little life that my beautiful firstborn daughter Amber had created. You're probably thinking by now that I'm a proper wuss! Maybe I am, but I've come to realise that as much as I adore Marla, the greatest joy has been watching Amber flourish in her new role as a mother.

I am beyond proud of her.

I'm beyond proud of them all.

The girls have grown up into beautiful women, inside and out. Don't get me wrong, we've all had our moments. The challenges of being a blended family have not passed us by, neither have teenage hormones, nor, for that matter, our own inadequacies as parents. But these girls make our hearts sing. They became a gang almost instantly, while Bekah and I were still working out what our relationship even was. When she was little, Maddie declared – long before I was convinced – that Bekah needed to bring her girls, and come and be the mummy in our house.

This gang is a force to be reckoned with. If you take one on, you take them all. And the noise when they're together can be overwhelming. Joyous, too.

That said, even though they can be so deeply unified, you couldn't find five more different characters, which has made parenting them just that bit more challenging. They are all funny – properly, comically funny – in their own ways.

Amber is the storyteller. She captivates the room, telling tales from the classroom where she works, or just from the general mishaps of her day. She leaves us in stitches.

Emmie is like a mini me, which I'm not entirely sure she'd take as a compliment. She shares my optimism and always has a smile on her face, ready to laugh at the funnier side of life. She is trained to look after horses, and works on a community farm helping young adults with learning disabilities. She is up with the sparrows, works phenomenally hard and loves what she does.

Maddie is our creative one. Using photos or videos, her ability to capture the beauty of the world around her is extraordinary.

She is also an amazing dancer and choreographer. We have loved watching her grow in confidence and kindness. She's still trying to work out what the future holds for her, but she's another hard worker, relentlessly chasing opportunities and coming back for more.

Gemma is one of my bonus daughters, if you understand what I mean. Gemma is the clever one – or 'The cleverist' as her Year Six end-of-school award said. The engraver at that trophy shop clearly needed to invest in a dictionary. She's a brilliant communicator, and I certainly haven't won an argument with her in a very long time. In fact, I'm smart enough to know not to even attempt it. I have marvelled at her skills in leading and speaking at church. She's so much better than I was at her age. She must get it from her mum.

And then there's Meg, the blonde child who was spoiling Bekah's tan that day when I first saw them across the pool. Meg is a peacemaker. She wants everyone to be okay. She worries about what people think and how they are, and takes responsibility for it all. She's studying to be a clinical psychologist. I'm always slightly concerned she's analysing my every move. I'm sure there'll be a dissertation out of it!

In July, we all went on holiday for a week. Bekah had been nervous about paying for a holiday in case I wasn't well enough to go, but some very kind friends, Trevor and Celia, offered us their home in Torbay and moved out to give us the roam of it.

We were blown away by their generosity.

And by their house!

That week was our first holiday together in nine years, so we resurrected old traditions. We laid on meals we'd always had on holiday. The girls played board games when the weather let us down (it was the British summer, after all – apparently, it's no respecter of summers of joy). They had a bake-off which led to much laughter… and more cake than you could shake a stick at. We even went on a boat trip.

It was just what we needed – to be together, with no pressure. We had plenty of good food and, best of all, a gorgeous baby girl to keep everyone occupied and delighted.

14
Staying alive

I had been offered the opportunity to receive a new course of immunotherapy, but I wasn't sure about it. We'd picked up along the way that this dual immunotherapy was a last-ditch attempt without much hope. Bekah and I were on the same page. We both felt the risks outweighed the benefits. We agreed that I'd just have the radiotherapy to keep my brain tumours at bay for as long as possible. As for the rest, we would let nature take its course, and I would enjoy feeling well for as long as possible.

We told the girls what we had decided, and they understood. I think we'd all been distressed at seeing my little brother David so ill. As a family, we agreed that quality of life was more important than quantity. I didn't want to be kept alive at all costs. I'd rather go quickly than have a long, lingering decline like my brother.

It's hard to imagine conversations like these if you've never had to have them. No one wants to sit and talk to the people they love about how they want to die or when to switch off life-support machines. But going through this has made us huge advocates of people having these kinds of conversations before it becomes a live issue.

We were united about not going ahead with the immunotherapy until we received a phone call from Sally. She'd heard that we had cancelled an appointment to go in for a session.

'What's the reason behind your decision?' she asked.

'Two things,' I said. 'The treatment isn't likely to make any difference, but it is likely to make me very ill.'

'That's true,' she said, 'and the reality is, the side effects may well be worse because of your diabetes. But there's an eight per cent chance of the immunotherapy working.'

'And where does that eight per cent get us?' Bekah asked. 'An extra three weeks? Months? What are we talking about?'

'I don't know for sure. Steve's type of melanoma is so rare, there's simply no data. But I do have some patients with the more ordinary melanoma who are still alive years after treatment.'

Now it was my turn. 'What would you do if you were in my shoes?' I asked.

Sally couldn't answer.

'We'll think about it,' we said.

As we boarded a tube to the Royal Marsden, we asked God to make it abundantly clear what we should do. And he did. As we went through the pre-op questionnaire, the doctor in charge of my radiotherapy asked, 'When are you starting immunotherapy?'

'We might not be.'

'In that case, I'm going to write "next week".'

'Why?'

'Because you can't have the stereotactic surgery on your brain if you don't attempt to control the rest of the cancer.'

That was the first signpost that it was right to have the surgery on my brain and to have immunotherapy.

The next came when I posted a photo on social media of the entrance to the CyberKnife department. I made a joke about it needing a less scary name. I proposed 'CyberThingy'. Various people added humorous responses, but one old friend commented that someone she knew had received this surgical procedure and, despite having only tolerated one round of immunotherapy, she was still going strong.

That settled it.

A few hours later, I received another, more accurate, brain scan – a procedure that involved me wearing a custom-fitted mesh mask moulded to keep my head and neck still. It was like a bespoke jelly mould, but without the joy of jelly at the end.

A week later, the day before King Charles's coronation, we returned for the CyberKnife procedure. As its name suggests, this was performed by a robot whose X-ray cameras monitor the position of the tumours before targeting them with multiple tiny radiotherapy beams, the precision of which lessens the chance of causing damage to healthy tissue. I wore my mask during this procedure – screwed to the table to hold me securely – and looked like something from the movie *Halloween*. Meanwhile, this futuristic machine delivered radiation not just to the three tumours we knew about, but to ten more that the latest scan had revealed. Some were microscopic. All were multiplying at an alarming rate.

While this was all painless, staying absolutely still for two-and-a-half hours was a challenge, especially with my bladder.

'Could you play some pop music?' I asked.

The songs helped me relax.

Well, most of them.

Before long, 'I Just Died in Your Arms Tonight' by Cutting Crew came on. Then there was Queen's 'Another One Bites the Dust'. Perhaps more encouraging was 'Staying Alive' by the Bee Gees.

As a veteran of hospital radio, I spoke to the radiation therapists afterwards about the choice of music. They were mortified. I thought it was hilarious. Having said that, if Bob Dylan had come on with 'Knockin' on Heaven's Door', I'd have been out of there.

Feeling a little sheepish, they gave me a coronation cupcake and took me to be reunited with the ever-present Bekah in the waiting room. I'd planned a little joke during my hours on the table. Well, what else was there to do?

I looked at Bekah quizzically. 'Who are you?' I asked.

It had all gone so smoothly in my imagination during the procedure. But when it came to it, I just couldn't keep a straight face long enough.

Everyone else in the waiting room found it hilarious.

Bekah was unmoved and merely rolled her eyes.

15

Where the sun don't shine

Midway through May, I started to feel pain in my back. To begin with, we put this down to me having lifted something badly. But as the days passed, Bekah began to question whether it could be linked to the tumour in my spine.

Bekah emailed Sally, asking if I could have some radiotherapy, noting that it would be a terrible shame to save my life, only for me to be paralysed. Perhaps they could stop me from being in pain before that became necessary.

The discomfort was rapidly worsening. I could no longer let Bekah rest her head on my shoulder when she got into bed. I was struggling to sit in most chairs. I couldn't lift anything heavier than the kettle. It was frightening, if I'm honest. Everything seemed to be declining very quickly.

Sally immediately sent me for another CT scan. This showed not only that the tumour had started crumbling my vertebrae, but that there was now a second tumour threatening to do the same lower down my spine. She booked me in for radiotherapy a fortnight later. In the meantime, she sent me home with paracetamol, ibuprofen, codeine and morphine, to be used as needed.

The next week, Bekah sensed God impressing on her to pray very specifically – to actually speak to my body.

'Remember who you are!' she said. Sitting in bed, she put one hand on my back and the other on my chest and told my immune system to wake up, to remember what it was created for, to recognise the tumours as the enemy and to tell them to get out, in Jesus' name.

Bekah wasn't used to praying like that, so it was a little awkward at first, but she kept doing it, day after day, and then she asked the 500-plus people in our private WhatsApp prayer group to pray the same thing in Jesus' name.

Two weeks later, when it was time to go in for my radiotherapy, Sally asked how much morphine I was taking.

'I haven't taken any painkillers for nearly a week,' I replied. 'Not even a paracetamol.'

She raised her eyebrows. 'Well, that's unexpected.'

I do like it when doctors are surprised. This began to give us hope that perhaps, in Jesus' name, we could continue to confound them.

In early May, we had returned to the Sussex Cancer Centre in Brighton to start a new combined immunotherapy of ipilimumab and nivolumab (try saying those quickly!). These block proteins that stop the immune system from working properly and also help the immune system find and kill cancer cells. This was administered through a drip into my arm.

We were aiming for four clear cycles of this combined immunotherapy, praying it wouldn't overstimulate my immune system into attacking the wrong thing. Sally was delighted with me as I headed into cycle four with nothing worse than some vitiligo – another case of friendly fire, which saw my immune system take out great patches of melanin from my skin, leaving me with symmetrical white marks on my hands, arms and head.

It was during this time that Bekah spotted what she calls a very beautiful patch on my back. Apparently, it looks like a pair of wings, just where she used to hold her hand and pray. It's probably just one of those things. Maybe I'd been drinking way too much Red Bull or, as I prefer to think, maybe it's a little reminder of God's goodness to us.

Wings aside, I had my fourth and final course of immunotherapy, and was already doing better than most people, tolerating the treatment like a pro. Three days after that fourth cycle, however, the wheels came off and the bottom fell out of my world. Or, more literally, the world fell out of my bottom.

I developed stage-three colitis seemingly overnight. My immune system had been attacking my colon, also known as the large intestine, and it had become inflamed, sensitive and angry. I was now feeling discomfort and pain in my tummy. This pain came and went, but it could be really horrible. I was going to the toilet seven times a day – more than that at night. On the plus side, I lost eight pounds of weight in one week.

Joking aside, it was serious.

We were due to head off to New Wine, a large Christian camping festival being held this year at the Kent Event Centre in Maidstone. I was down to do an after-hours show. Bekah and I had also booked the *Sorted* and Restored stands in the marketplace for the fortnight. I was adamant we should still go. Bekah gave me a stern talking to about the realities of a fortnight at a festival with a stomach doing what mine was doing. She made me promise to ring the hospital before we left.

Of course, they didn't want me going anywhere without seeing them, so we packed the car with props and display materials, and headed to Kent via the Brighton cancer centre to see the immunotherapy toxicity team. They were fabulous. They pumped a high dose of methylprednisolone into me via a drip. This is a potent anti-inflammatory agent known as a corticosteroid. Corticosteroids are used to treat many inflammatory diseases, such as my colitis. It had an almost instant effect, and I felt like Superman as we headed to New Wine.

Things were going great. We had lots of good conversations on the *Sorted* stand, we got some new subscriptions, and we almost sold out of the 'Our God Rains' golf umbrellas after several heavy downpours in the first few days. My late-night performance went down a storm during a storm – with 500 crammed into the venue to enjoy my 'Tricks and Laughs' show, and another 200 turned away. If laughter is a great medicine, then making people laugh is like a super drug. I felt almost back to normal.

But the steroids gradually began to wear off and the colitis returned with a vengeance. Once again, I felt terrible. I was back to using the toilet endlessly and being up a lot in the night. I felt listless and lifeless as my body stopped absorbing any nutrients. I have never been so glad to be in a hotel and not camping.

I didn't sleep much. My diabetes was turbocharged by the steroids, which meant I had insanely high blood sugar for days. This was followed by two nights with severe hypos – an abnormally low level of glucose in my blood. When your glucose level is too low, your body doesn't have enough energy to carry out its regular functions. Normally, a couple of jelly babies and a biscuit would normalise me, but on both occasions these hypos lasted hours, and I was in and out of consciousness.

It was time for drastic action.

Bekah force-fed me an entire bag of jelly babies, some orange juice, several cookies, and a piece of toast and honey in the wee hours of the morning, all scrambled together by the wonderful late-night staff at the Orida hotel. Bekah engineered all this while talking on the phone to a 999 operator. I honestly think I'd have been found in a coma by the cleaning staff the next morning without this impromptu medical team. Eventually, my sugar levels came back to normal, but Bekah stayed awake all night watching to see what was happening.

I felt so sick that week, but, being Mr Positive, I was grateful the hotel's designers had placed the toilet so close to the bath. This meant I could simultaneously use the toilet while being sick in the bath. Who said men can't multitask?

Our home medical team arranged for us to visit the local hospital for a few days in a row for some further steroid infusions, but eventually we were left with no choice but to admit defeat and leave New Wine a few days into the second week. The boys on the other stands helped Bekah pack up while I rested. I felt so terrible. I secretly wondered if this was the beginning of the end.

We began making daily visits to the Royal Sussex County Hospital when we returned, which inevitably ended up taking hours longer than we hoped. The Emergency Ambulatory Care Unit (EACU) became our second home for the next couple of weeks, and we only went home to sleep. I sat with drips of steroids and various nutrients for up to fourteen hours a day. My blood sugars were yoyoing. The only reason they let me home at all was that Bekah's maths skills and rapidly growing medical understanding meant she could just about keep up with the constant recalibration of my insulin ratios. It was a big pressure for her, though. The situation was taking its toll on both of us.

There was some unexpected excitement at one point during the relentless tedium of drips and hospital food.

'We're sending you upstairs for a flexible sigmoidoscopy,' they said.

That sounded quite interesting until they explained what it would involve. I soon decided that tedium has its upside.

When I arrived, a nurse checked my temperature, blood pressure, breathing and heart rate.

'Are you allergic to anything?' she asked.

'No.'

That didn't seem good enough.

'Are you allergic to anything?'

'No.'

After what felt like the hundredth time, I said, 'Cats.'

She duly wrote that down. Then she left me in a side room for an hour while she went to lunch.

At this point, everyone else involved in my care thought I was lost.

I'd been given a flimsy floral hospital gown to change into and some paper shorts. These had an opening at the back. I didn't fancy wandering back to reception dressed like that to find out what was happening. Eventually, the nurse returned to give me an enema, so the endoscopist would have a clear view of my bowel (another sentence I never thought I'd write in a book). The hospital had written in advance to suggest that a friend or relative insert the enema in the privacy of my own home.

You have got to be joking, I remember thinking to myself. *That's what I pay my taxes for. I'll get a nurse to do it at the hospital.*

I was shown into the procedure room, where I lay on a bed on my left side, my knees tucked up to my chest. That surprised me for starters. I hadn't realised I was so flexible.

Little pleasures.

They put cold gel on the colonoscope to make it more comfortable. Then the endoscopist poked it slowly and carefully where the sun don't shine, up into my large bowel.

Not so pleasurable.

It was a strange but painless sensation. I watched the entire procedure with fascination on the TV monitor. During the test, they took photographs of my bowel lining and some tissue samples (biopsies). I was grateful for the technology. I dreaded to think how big the cameras were fifty years ago. Those VHS cameras were massive back in the day. But in the end, the whole procedure wasn't nearly as bad or embarrassing as I'd feared.

We all laughed at one point when the theatre radio started playing a song by Barry White. 'My First, My Last, My Everything'.

'I'll never be able to listen to Barry White romantically again,'

I commented.

It could have been worse. They could have played Labi Siffre's 'Something Inside So Strong'.

Three weeks into the steroid treatment, it was clear that it wasn't making anything better, so Sally talked us through the remaining options. Doing nothing wasn't an option. But much more of this and I'd die anyway.

I was given a dose of immunosuppressants, which seemed counterintuitive after spending the last three months trying to awaken my immune system. But there wasn't much choice. It was another day and another drip. This time, however, it was like someone had waved a magic wand. Our prayers were answered. The colitis cleared up as quickly as it had started.

16

My B-positive brain

'How do you remain so positive?' people ask me.

That's a good question. There's a part of me that thinks I may well have been born this way – that my blood type is B-positive. I was always cheery as a kid, and I still seem to have that kind of personality, whatever the circumstances. My glass has always been half full. I'm an eternal optimist. Maybe this positivity is in my genes. We'll come back to this thought later, because it's complicated.

There's another part of me that knows this is not just the way I'm wired. When I look at my whole life, rather than just these last two years, the biggest contributing factor to my positivity has been my Christian faith. My faith is everything to me. Without it, I might well have ended up with a very different outlook. This book might have ended up as a misery memoir (yes, that is an actual genre).

Like many of you reading this book, I wasn't brought up in a Christian family. My faith journey started when I noticed an intriguing sign on a noticeboard at our school. It was way back in the days before O levels and work started to encroach on my life; in the days when summer holidays seemed to stretch out over an eternity of sand-filled hair and ice cream. The poster at our secondary school was advertising a new Boys' Brigade (BB) company starting up just five minutes from our house. Enticed by the lure of football, as well as the promise of joint activities with the Girls' Brigade, I decided to give it a try.

The Boys' Brigade was founded by a Scottish businessman and former soldier called William Alexander Smith. He held the first meeting in a church hall in Glasgow in 1883, inviting boys from his Sunday school along. His goal was to advance God's kingdom among boys, and the Brigade is still going strong all over the world 140 years later.

Our local Boys' Brigade company was affiliated with a church so dull there was more life in the graveyard. Not to be deterred, I went along to the Friday night meetings with my mates and enjoyed them. I was thirteen, and hadn't a worry in the world.

I'll never forget the summer of 1980. It seemed to last from April to September. In July, we headed off on BB camp. Our mums packed our suitcases with a spare pair of pants, a toothbrush and some money for the tuck shop (they were very small suitcases). More than seventy of us piled into the coach in Bournemouth and headed down to sleepy Devon.

We stayed in Axmouth, a quaint little village with trams and a pretty harbour, just down the road from Lyme Regis. It was idyllic. We spent all day hanging around our Green Ridge tents, listening to Blondie and Bad Manners on the radio, kicking a football around, swimming in the sea, and playing pranks on our pals.

Which brings me to my mate Nigel.

Some other mates and I had invented a terrifying fictional character we called 'Axmouth Eddie' – an axe-wielding maniac who scoured the town by day and night, or so we claimed. Inspired by the Christian meetings we were having in the evenings, we told the younger lads the only way to protect themselves from Eddie's assaults was to wear the sign of the cross on their bodies. This would ward off the evil man.

Leading by example, we found some masking tape and sellotaped a massive cross to each of our chests. The younger lads followed suit. One very hot day, we visited the beach as a group, oblivious to the other holidaymakers who were staring at our chests.

It was a scorcher of a day and my mate Nigel, desperate to cool himself down, trundled off by himself in search of an ice cream. While he was gone, the rest of us decided to head back to camp. I grabbed Nigel's bag and took it with us to keep it safe. It was years before mobile phones were invented, so poor old Nigel spent half the day scouring the beach – first for his mates and then for his bag. Then it dawned on him. He'd gone from beached to deserted.

Nigel turned up at the camp a few hours later wearing nothing but his swimming trunks. He was dehydrated and somewhat delirious. His arrival caused a stir. He bore a striking resemblance to a lobster, and we could feel the heat radiating from his crimson body from fifty paces. Standing in just his Speedos, he was swiftly slathered with calamine lotion. Told to remove the taped cross, he winced as he gingerly pulled it from his chest.

Then we saw it. Emblazoned in purest white from neck to navel, from nipple to nipple, was a huge cross, standing out starkly against his sunburned skin. It must have been agony that night trying to find a position in his sleeping bag that didn't hurt.

There was some good news for poor Nigel, though. Branded so visibly with the sign of the cross, he would be perfectly safe from Axmouth Eddie for weeks, if not months. It took a few days, but Nigel eventually recovered and forgave us.

What I remember most from that week was not Nigel, however, but a vicar called Bruce who played the accordion and told us about Jesus. Each night after supper we sat in the big white marquee – aka the Mess Tent – singing songs about God and hearing how much he loved us. Bruce really knew God and told us about him in a language we understood. He brought faith to life in a unique way. At last I had met someone who was excited about being a Christian.

Bruce explained that being a Christian meant more than going to church on Sunday and wearing sandals (with socks). I heard about a heavenly Father who loved me so much he sent his Son to die on the cross for me. I learned that God wanted to be my friend.

It was Bruce who gave me a booklet called *Journey into Life* by Norman Warren. He seemed to have a job lot of them. The booklet explained in very simple terms how we had all done wrong and needed to get right with God through a friendship with his Son, Jesus. Reading this completely blew my mind.

Coming from a family that didn't attend church, and going to a youth group at a church that was barely breathing, I had never heard this before. This camp changed my life in a way that nothing else could have done. I am eternally grateful to the men and woman – including the amazing camp cook, Miss Smith – who gave up their time to run it for us. Their sacrifice and commitment provided me and the other boys with a chance to encounter God and turn our lives around.

It was here, among the sunburn, the sea and the smell of chemical toilets, that I decided to follow Jesus for the rest of my days. It was the best decision of my life.

When the camp ended, we caught the coach back to Bournemouth. As soon as we got home, I dumped my suitcase in the kitchen, ran upstairs to my room, got down on my knees and said the prayer at the back of *Journey into Life*. I prayed it with all my heart, asking God to come into my life and take over.

Things have never been the same since. From that moment on, the cross hasn't been gaffer-taped onto my chest, but it has been imprinted on my heart and soul. I truly believe that Jesus Christ paid for all my sins on the cross, and that, thanks to his amazing, sacrificial love, I am forgiven.

Not only that, but I am also assured that I will spend eternity with him in heaven. Like Nigel, the impression of the cross has never left me. It is as powerful today as it was then. Throughout my teenage years and beyond, I have never lost my faith in him.

When I left school, I decided to apply for a job in a bank. Not many people from Kingsleigh went to university, so knowing someone who worked in the recruitment department at Barclays Bank, I put in an application. And I got the job.

My mum proudly declared, 'It's a job for life. Banks never close or lay off staff.'

She's a wonderful woman, but long-term forecasting was never one of her strengths. The technical revolution has since proved her wrong.

I continued attending our small church and volunteering as a steward at places like Spring Harvest. I didn't feel I had many talents, but I knew I could move chairs. I also enjoyed having a walkie-talkie in my back pocket and thought – even if I say so myself – I looked especially dashing in a fluorescent yellow tabard.

One night, a preacher called Philip Mohabir was speaking in the Big Top. 'God's calling people here into full-time Christian work,' he cried. It was as if he was speaking directly to me.

A year or so later I resigned from Barclays and started the adventure I've been on for more than thirty-five years: adopting creative ways to communicate the good news of Jesus.

To be a bit different, I started off using escapology as a visual parable of how things in our lives can tie us up, but explaining that God can set us free. I'd travel the world with a case full of chains, handcuffs and a straitjacket. That was then.

These days I do comedy magic. If you don't find it funny, it's just magic. Of course, it's not real magic, it's just tricks. I'd hate you to think I'm into dodgy stuff and burn this book – especially if you're in a bookshop and haven't paid for it yet.

My occupation does raise a few eyebrows when I introduce myself to new people. Even Bekah laughed when I first told her what I did for a living.

'No, really. What do you do?'

'I'm a magician,' I insisted. 'I use tricks to communicate the Christian message to young and old. I go all over the place.'

In fulfilling God's call on my life, there's never been a steady income or much job security, but God has been so good to me. When there hasn't been enough money to get a big shop in at Sainsbury's, a box of food has appeared on our doorstep or vouchers have been pushed through the letterbox.

Once, during an especially fraught time, I sat at my kitchen table, head in hands, totally despondent. I was three years into a Christmas animation project designed to show the true meaning of Christmas in cartoon form with a host of celebrities providing the voices. It was called *It's a Boy!* I was planning to send a copy to every primary school in the UK, but it was proving to be a tough journey. I had no idea how I was going to finance its completion.

Then the post arrived. The first letter I opened was from an organisation that had supported me for years. Enclosed was a cheque for £20,000 towards the project. The note with it read: 'We want to let you know that we support you in all that you are doing. You're doing a fantastic job. Keep going.'

I'm not embarrassed to admit that I became emotional when I read those words.

Then I got up, and I kept going.

I've been performing since 1988, and I love it. Standing on stage, telling people about Jesus, making them laugh and performing are some of my favourite things. I'm passionate about communicating the gospel in ways that people understand. I love showing people of all ages that the Christian faith is relevant to their lives, and that being a Christian is not about going to church twenty-five times on a Sunday, watching *Songs of Praise* and helping old ladies across the road – even if they don't want to go. I love using magic and humour to demonstrate a point. I consider myself truly blessed because every day I get to do what I enjoy most.

It hasn't always been easy, but I've never regretted making the choice to do it. I have many questions to ask God some day, but the one thing I can be sure of when the goalposts seem to be moving around is that God knows exactly what is going on. Psalm 139:13 assures us that before we were born, God knew every day that we would live, and he reminds us in Jeremiah 29:11: 'I know the plans I have for you... plans to prosper you and not to harm you.' That's a promise.

Perhaps you can see why I'm a B-positive person. I found faith in Jesus when I was thirteen, and that faith has encouraged me to believe positive things. As the old saying goes, 'I may not know what the future holds, but I do know who holds the future: Jesus.'

But there's something else I need to share. I said at the start of this chapter that I was born cheery. It's in my genes. I also said it's complex. It's complex in the sense that I'm perhaps a little different from others when it comes to the way my brain works. Some of you are probably thinking this already, so it may not come as big news. But I want to be authentic in my account of the last two years. I want you to see my personality the way my wife does.

She thinks I'm genetically wired to be positive. What does she mean by that?

Bekah recalls that when I was sent home with my 'Understanding Melanoma' booklet back in April 2022, I didn't read it for a long time. When I finally did, I was gobsmacked.

'There are pages and pages in here about how this might make me feel,' I told her. 'Do other people think these things?'

She laughed.

'Why are you laughing?'

'Because I've known for a very long time that you don't experience the world like me or most people.'

Fast-forward to a year later, April 2023. We had just seen our oncologist. For the next few days, I was devastated. These were the first tears I had shed. For the very first time, I was forced to face the reality of what was happening to me. Bekah had been in that same place for the past eighteen months. I'd been stoical up to that point, but now I was overwhelmed. It had taken all that time for me to let my feelings take precedence over my thoughts.

While this was hard for me, it was a relief for my wife. As she puts it: 'In truth it was a blessing for me, because we were finally on the same page, walking the same path together. I'd been carrying the weight and the worry, and the girls' emotions, for a long time, partly to protect Steve. Now we could do it as a team.'

This is important, because my positivity doesn't just come down to my faith in Jesus. It's also a symptom of the way my brain works. Bekah reckons I have a level of autism which makes my way of navigating these experiences quite unique. And as has so often been true in the past, she's right. But I like to think of my neurodivergence as my superpower!

17

Twin-track living

I wrote about my positivity in the last chapter, but I don't want you to think I'm one of those people who pretend the sun is always shining and that there are never any dark skies. That's totally unrealistic unless you live in Iceland for half the year. I'm very realistic now about what we're facing. Since receiving the news that I had five months left, we've been living with a strange mixture of hospitals and holidays, moments of sadness and memories of joy. In fact, there's been light and shade at every turn.

On the one hand, we believe that God can do miracles and that he's able to heal me of every trace of cancer. That's faith. On the other, we were told on 17 April that I have an incurable illness and there's only a short amount of time left. That's realism. Bekah calls this twin-track living. Our wheels are wedded to both faith and realism. It's about believing in miracles as well as preparing for my death.

This is like straddling two worlds at the same time. In one you're preparing yourself and the family for the worst; in the other you're holding on to the hope that God will step in and change the story. He's very good at that sort of thing. There have been no voices from heaven telling us that I'm going to be healed or that I'm going to die. How are you supposed to order your life when you simply don't know?

In the absence of any blinding lights (outside of those found in hospitals) and resounding voices from heaven, we chose to begin the process of doing the practical tasks associated with the end of life. This started with a call to our life insurance company. Bekah once again stepped into the breach, determined to shield me. She took the phone into the other room, but I could hear her voice breaking as she told the person at the other end that her husband had been given five months to live, and again as she answered the formal questions that ensued.

What a horrible job that poor person on the other end of the phone had. Bekah says she was the kindest, gentlest lady. Imagine having conversations with people going through the worst moments of their life. Imagine doing that every day. What a tough gig... but what a calling. What an opportunity to take the edge off the pain people endure. And that's what she did. Her kindness helped us navigate a road we never wanted to walk. It would take a couple of months for the process to end, but this was something we'd been dreading. We no longer needed to.

Next came the appointment at our local hospice to discuss end-of-life care. I think this was one of the worst days of my life. For years, I'd entertained the kids at Chestnut Tree House hospice in Worthing every Christmas. It was always a tear-jerker as dozens of beautiful children filed in to watch me do a magic show. I was always an emotional wreck before and after (that won't surprise you by now), but I managed to pull myself together to cheer up these precious youngsters, most of whom had just weeks to live.

Now it was my turn.

I was being invited to the adult version, St Barnabas House

hospice, also in Worthing. Only I wasn't going there to entertain the residents. I was going to discuss my own life-limiting illness and end-of-life care. This was tough for Bekah, too. She'd worked for a local church and visited the hospice with her pastor's hat on. This was a place filled with memories of supporting families through their last moments with loved ones.

She knew what going there meant.

Although I was filled with trepidation, the place turned out to be quite remarkable. Set in beautifully maintained grounds, each patient had a private garden area so they could have their doors open all year round, listening to the trickling from the water features and the sound of birdsong.

Surprisingly, we found that it wasn't a depressing place at all, and the staff were doing an extraordinary job in supporting adults with life-limiting illnesses, along with their loved ones, so they could all enjoy life as fully as possible in the time they had left.

In some ways, this was like any other medical appointment, except this time we were being asked about priorities. Which was our priority: quality or quantity of life? Who would make medical decisions if I couldn't any more? Where did I want to die: in the hospice or at home? Bekah and I had already talked about these thing. With her newfound superpower of being able to hold it together when it mattered, she answered the questions, occasionally stopping to check with me that she was saying the right thing.

I knew that, if it was at all possible, I didn't want to end my days in this hospice, however lovely it was. I wanted to be with my family and my dog, in my own home. So long as it didn't become too much of a burden for my loved ones, I wanted to be in my familiar surroundings with those I adored. All this was written down.

Then, in an unexpected but very welcome gearshift, the woman interviewing us said, 'I'm going to discharge you back to your GP for now. Honestly, you're far too well to be under our care.'

When she'd finished talking with us, she asked if we would like a blue badge for our car. This elusive piece of cardboard helps disabled people park closer to their destination. It also often enables people to park without paying. Every cloud has a silver lining, I guess.

Having seen Bekah do so much for me, I decided to organise a funeral plan on my own. We'd had so much money raised for us, and it was time to get it done. I think organising my brother's funeral had traumatised me. I didn't want my girls to go through that.

I decided not to organise a traditional funeral. I felt it was a real waste of £8,000. Instead, I chose a direct cremation plan. The company takes care of everything from the moment a deceased loved one is collected until the ashes are returned to the family. There is no need for a funeral. My ashes would be scattered at the beach, and it would only cost £1,300.

I did, however, plan a thanksgiving service for a month later, once the dust (as it were) had settled, for family, friends, colleagues and neighbours to come and remember and celebrate. With the money we had saved on the funeral, everyone would be able to enjoy some of my favourite things – coffee, cake and prosecco – after the service. I figured with the extra money they could get plenty of all three, providing we avoided Waitrose. Maybe there would even be enough left over to pay for a bench down on the beach. I think I'd like that. That same week I recorded a podcast with my buddy, Simon Guillebaud, to be played after my passing.

The last of the preparations involved sorting our wills. Someone came over to talk through our options. It was another tough conversation with a lot of talk about safeguarding legacies in the event of a future partner for Bekah. We held it together while this stranger took notes, but once he was gone, Bekah lost it and just sobbed.

'I don't want a future partner,' she cried.

I hugged her and said, 'I don't want that either. I just want it to be us.'

We held each other tight that evening, Bekah silently crying till she finally went to bed and fell asleep. This conversation had just been too much, too close to the bone. The weight of all these preparations had finally ground us down.

But they were finally over, and we could start living again. We could take the paperwork, the wills and the powers of attorney, and just tuck them in a drawer and forget about them. Hopefully for many years to come.

It was time to get busy living.

But one thing was still bothering Bekah. This won't come as a surprise to many of you, but she thinks about things far more deeply than I do. She admitted that she had been lying awake at night worrying about all these plans.

'Are we somehow showing a lack of faith in God? That I've given up on you?'

In my inimitable way, I said, 'Don't be daft, babe.'

That didn't seem to make things any better.

Fortunately, in his inimitable way, God got through to her far more effectively. We'd started listening to the *Bible in One Year* by Nicky Gumbel each morning. That day, we settled with a cup of coffee (me) and tea (her) and listened to the Bible reading. It was John 20 – the story of Mary Magdalene going to the tomb after Jesus had died. She planned to perform the practical and customary task of anointing his body for burial. But when she arrived, Mary didn't find Jesus in the tomb. She didn't understand what had happened to him.

Then Jesus, risen from the dead, came to her. Even then, she didn't understand. She didn't recognise him. She only realised it was Jesus when he called her by name.

Bekah took my hand as we listened, the tears flowing again. But this time she was smiling.

'Mary was just doing what she knew to do with the information she had at the time,' she said.

I looked on blankly.

As I frequently do.

'Mary planned for Jesus' death,' she said, 'but it didn't stop him rising again. Her actions didn't mean she lacked faith. They weren't wrong, either. She was honouring Jesus the only way she knew how, and that was okay.'

Even I could see what this meant. With God's help, you can do twin-track living. You can be practical as well as spiritual. You can be realistic and also full of faith. You can prepare for the worst without ceasing to believe for the best.

That was an epiphany.

Mary set her mind to fulfil the task of anointing Jesus's body, but she never denied the possibility of a miracle occurring. She was modelling what it meant to run on two tracks.

So right now, our little train is rumbling along the twin tracks of living in joy and pain in parallel. We're planning for the worst with the information we've been given, but we're also holding out for the best – for an encounter with Jesus that would change everything.

We don't plan on stopping until we reach our destination. In the meantime, we fully intend to enjoy the buffet cart en route.

We've got busy living.

Even if it's twin-track living.

18

Just do it

Back in January 2022, when I had just had the operation on my foot, Bekah was speaking at our wonderful home church, All Saints in Littlehampton. Her sermon was part of a wider series on sharing our faith with others. She had been asked to speak about sharing hope.

She played a clip from a favourite TV show of mine. It's another strange confession you're about to hear, but this hit series might have become a favourite of yours, too, if you'd been living with six women like me.

I'm referring, of course, to *Desperate Housewives*.

The clip in question showed one of the housewives, Lynette, surprising another, Bree, by asking if she can come to her church.

Eventually, Lynette – a hurricane and breast cancer survivor – starts asking Bree some of life's big questions about strife and suffering. She wants to know how Bree's faith helped her get through her troubles.

Bree is embarrassed. She stutters and stumbles, and doesn't have an answer, which is criminal really, because how often do we get such an open goal to talk about our faith?

In her sermon, Bekah talked about sharing our faith with those around us by helping them to see how it brings hope when times are hard. She shared some of our story so far, including her worries about finances, and how God had provided. So far, so victorious.

'The thing is,' she continued, 'I don't know what the future holds. I don't know what the test results are going to be, but I do know this: God is good. All the time. And it will be okay. It might not be the okay I would choose, but God will still be good, and it will still be okay.'

Bekah's voice broke as she said that, and a little bit of me did, too. I was watching online at home in my PJs, enjoying a mug of steaming hot coffee with my poorly foot elevated.

She had articulated something I wasn't sure I wanted to hear but knew I had to confront: 'How can we be okay when nothing is okay?' This was more challenging than, 'It's okay not to be okay.' That's good as far as it goes. This was something deeper still.

I'm a simple man, and sometimes I struggle to find the words to talk about complex emotions and complex questions, and how these two connect. My family will attest to that. They're all tons better at that sort of thing than I am. Bekah, however, has a knack for bringing together her emotional intelligence and her theological understanding, and helping people journey with her in faith. God seemed to be supernaturally feeding her lines that were designed as much for us as a family as for those in the congregation.

Her next sermon was about the unshakeable kingdom of God. She was preaching from Hebrews 12 this time. This chapter starts by talking about running the race of faith, and it finishes by describing the world we live in as one that is shaken, and that will be shaken. The writer concludes: 'We are receiving a kingdom that cannot be shaken,' alluding to the unshakeable kingdom of God.

Everyone who chooses to believe in Jesus is a part of this kingdom. All you need to do in order to enter it and live there is to have faith in him. Once we believe in Jesus, we start to find our peace, joy and well-being in the security this kingdom offers. We start to know where our true home is, where we really belong, in an unshakeable kingdom. This kingdom will stand forever. Isn't that profound?

Knowing we belong to a kingdom that cannot be shaken makes a huge difference to our attitude. Paul wrote this while he was in prison: 'I have learned the secret of being content in any and every situation, whether well fed or hungry, whether living in plenty or in want. I can do all this through him [Jesus] who gives me strength' (Philippians 4:12-13). Those are the words of a man who knew what life was like in an unshakable kingdom.

Paul understood what it meant to be okay when nothing is okay. He truly knew what it meant to live in peace and contentment, even in dire circumstances. This is a kingdom you can inhabit even while you're in a hospital room, a Roman cell or a hospice office. This is a kingdom that provides security in danger, contentment in chaos, and peace when the world around you is shaking. This kingdom doesn't always change your external situations, but it does offer you the opportunity to change your internal responses. It's a comforting reminder that however wild the winds blow, however stormy our world becomes, there is something deeper that still holds firm and will never be shaken.

These are easy words to say or write, but I want to get busy living in the truth of them. What does this kind of lifestyle look like? How did Paul become so content? How can I live like this when the test results don't go the way I hope, when we don't know how we're going to pay the next set of bills, when I can't even get out of my seat or protect my wife and kids from the pain they are experiencing?

The answer, of course, is Jesus.

It generally is.

A Sunday school teacher once asked her class, 'What's got a bushy tail, is red and likes to eat nuts?'

A child raised her hand. 'Well, it sounds like a squirrel to me, Miss, but I know the answer must be Jesus.'

You've probably heard that one.

The answer truly is Jesus. He's the king of the unshakable kingdom.

Bekah and I have become more intentional about starting our day with Jesus – a practice that had slipped, if I'm honest. It's pretty simple, really. We listen to the Bible and Nicky Gumbel over our morning cuppa in bed, and then we talk about what we noticed in the reading. Then we pray.

We listen to Christian podcasts in the car – ones that help us to know Jesus better. We take time to sit and notice the beauty around us, the gifts from God we had previously taken for granted: the West Sussex downs, a stunning sunset, birds singing in the trees. I've even begun to appreciate seagulls, unless I'm eating a bag of chips at the beach. In that case, they are still dastardly winged thieves.

Then there's sharing my story. There's nothing like being given five months to live to focus your mind. It's made me think about what kind of legacy I want to leave. By legacy, I don't mean something financial in a will. I mean the message I want the world to hear. A message about what's unshakable: namely, Jesus and his kingdom. I want to impact the world with my story about what really matters.

That first weekend after receiving my prognosis, Bekah and I drove to Norfolk so I could get back to gigging. I did my usual routine on the Sunday morning at the family service, but my friend Nick, the pastor, told me to say whatever was on my heart at the end. It wasn't the most profound thing I'd ever said. It was simply this: 'Just do it.'

I talked about the things we put off until we're in a more secure position – when the mortgage is paid, or when the kids have grown up and left home. I talked about the decisions we delay because they feel too big or we feel too inadequate. And I talked about how all this changes when you're told you have five months left to live, and you realise there's no time to wait. So I told them all, 'Just do it.'

I've been just doing it ever since – following wherever God leads me, speaking out the words I believe he has given me and challenging those I meet to think about what they'd do differently if they knew they only had five months to live. I've been encouraging people to get busy living... even if, like us, that involves twin-track living. Just do it.

At the 1992 Barcelona Olympics, British athlete Derek Redmond had one last chance to compete in an Olympic final. All he needed to do was finish among the top four runners in his 400m semifinal and he'd be through to the final. His dream was about to be fulfilled.

Then, mid-race, disaster struck.

His hamstring snapped.

All the other runners overtook him as he hobbled towards the finish line on his one remaining good leg. His dream was in tatters. His career was over. His chance had evaporated.

Then something extraordinary happened.

A short, well-upholstered man in a T-shirt, shorts and baseball cap climbed over the fence and ran alongside him.

This was Jim Redmond.

Derek's father.

Jim put his arm around his son's shoulder and walked him all the way to the finish line. It is said that the ovation they were given was louder and more heartfelt than was heard for any winner at the '92 Games.

Afterwards, when Jim was interviewed, he shared how he had been part of his son's whole athletic journey, and wasn't about to let him go out like this. 'We're going to finish this together,' he told his boy.[6] His baseball cap had three words emblazoned on it: 'Just do it!'

The Nike sports brand logo.

The word 'nike' comes from an ancient Greek word that means 'victory' or 'winning'. Just as Derek had Jim, we all have a loving Father in heaven who will jump over any wall to help us 'just do it'. He may not fix the hamstring, but he will enable us to finish the race. The true winners in life are those who walk with their Father across the finishing line.

I doubt whether Derek Redmond ever imagined that his legacy to the world would be this inspiring image of fatherly love and perseverance. He probably thought it would be winning a medal. But sometimes victory is not about standing on a podium; it's about limping through a stadium with your Father at your side.

This book you're reading is a 'Just do it' venture. It's an act of 'nike' faith – of conquering and winning. Paul, the same man who found himself in jail in Philippians 4, had this to say at the end of Romans 8: 'We are more than conquerors through him who loved us' (Romans 8:37).

The English phrase 'more than conquerors' is just one word in the original Greek. It's the verb *hypernikao*. The word 'nike' is in there somewhere. We are more than winners when we live in the love of our heavenly Father.

So remember the baseball cap.

And the logo.

Remember Derek Redmond's dad.

And the lengths he went to for his son.

While you have time.

Just do it!

---

[6] S. Burnton, '50 stunning Olympic moments No3: Derek Redmond and dad finish 400m', *The Guardian*, 30 November 2011: https://www.theguardian.com/sport blog/2011/nov/30/50-stunning-olympic-moments-derek-redmond (accessed 7 November 2023).

19

It's *where*, not *why*

One of the things most people do when they're given a terminal diagnosis is to ask the question why. 'Why me? What have I done to deserve this?' And perhaps the most common question is: 'if God is love, as Christians claim he is, then why is he allowing me to go through this? If he has the power to erase every trace of my cancer, why doesn't he do it?'

I certainly don't want to devalue the importance of these questions in any way. People who are going through severe sickness and suffering have every reason, and maybe every right, to protest. But it's not for me.

I have never once asked why. Others have on my behalf. I've done loads of interviews about my cancer journey, and it comes up all the time. When they ask, 'Why you?' I answer, 'Why not me?' and sometimes cheekily add, 'Cancer is an equal opportunities disease.'

That usually raises a wry smile.

You may think I'm a bit odd in this regard, but then I did share what my wife thinks about my autistic brain in the last chapter.

I'm convinced I'm genetically preconditioned in a particular – or some might say *peculiar* – way. Maybe 'divinely designed' is better. I like that. Or 'neurologically wired'. Maybe my brain is a strange mixture of all three.

But we also need to factor in my Christian faith. Ever since I decided to follow Jesus at the age of thirteen, I've had this childlike trust in God that whatever I need to go through in life, he will be with me, whether those experiences are happy or sad.

I've always had this assurance that Jesus knows what's best for me. If the road turns out to be rough and more than a little steep, I know he's going to be there, walking with me, never leaving me for a second.

For me, the question is therefore less about *why*, and more about *where*. It's not so much, 'Why is Jesus allowing this?' It's more about, 'Where can I see signs of his presence?'

After all, didn't he promise he would always stay with those who chose to follow him?

Just before he left his friends, Jesus promised he would send the Holy Spirit, and that he would therefore be with them forever (John 14:16). That's why he said: 'And be sure of this: I am with you always, even to the end of the age' (Matthew 28:20, NLT).

Does this mean Jesus has walked with me as I've gone through the journey described in this book? The answer is a resounding yes. The thing that is so unique and wonderful about Jesus is this: he endured the worst physical and mental suffering in what is often referred to as his Passion (his suffering before and during the cross).

He has travelled a sorrowful road himself, and is therefore intimately acquainted with our grief. He has been through the ordeal of dying and death, and is therefore personally familiar with the grim challenges of our all-too-human mortality. He has truly walked where we walk.

Many people don't realise how unique this is in the context of religious belief and human philosophy. It's profound. Christianity is the only system of belief which teaches its followers that God has been through what we are going through; that he has suffered what we are suffering; that he has even been through the torment of death and passed through the gates of hell.

In Jesus, God is uniquely revealed as the One who suffers with us when we suffer. He is not absent, aloof, angry or apathetic when we experience hell on earth. When we go through pain, he is there. He is with us. He is on the road with us, saying, 'I am here. Don't worry. Together, we've got this. Just keep going, my child.'

I have always believed this.

I continue to believe it.

And I will believe it up to my last breath.

Whenever you go to a funeral, I can guarantee that you will either read or sing Psalm 23. This was originally a song of praise in which King David compared God to a shepherd who leads his sheep down paths both easy and dangerous. During this song, David makes the simple statement: 'Your rod and your staff, they comfort me.'

But what does this mean?

Well, you've come to the right man for the answer. You probably don't know this, but I became something of a sheep expert back in the day when I co-presented a live ITV Sunday morning show with Gloria Hunniford, aptly named *Sunday*.

One of my favourite memories was interviewing a world champion sheep shearer, and then having a go myself. I'm not sure who looked more terrified, me or the sheep. The night before the close shave, I'd lain awake in my hotel room, trying to learn as many sheep facts as I could – acutely aware that the usual suggestion for overcoming insomnia is to count sheep. It certainly didn't work for me, but I did learn a thing or two about sheep and shepherds.

Back in Jesus' day, whenever the route was treacherous, a shepherd would go ahead of the sheep. He would take his rod and staff, and tap the rocks along the way. He did this to reassure the sheep – many of whom could not see him – that he was still there. He was still leading them, they were still in good hands and it was only a matter of time before they found themselves back in their pen.

I doubt if it's possible to find a more comforting picture when you're going down a pathway that looks, to all intents and purposes, as if it's going to end in death. When we do that, we may not be able to see Jesus, the Good Shepherd, with our physical eyes, but we can hear the reassuring tap-tap-tapping of his staff.

Let me share some moments when Bekah and I have heard, as it were, these reassuring sounds.

When we went to the Royal Marsden, we were anxious about finding somewhere to park. I know that sounds like a trivial thing in the grand scheme of things, but sometimes it's these micro stresses that can tip me over the edge. The hospital is in the centre of London, and parking is a real challenge. There really is nowhere to park.

But during our first visit, as we walked from the tube station to the hospital, I realised we'd been there years before, filming with Care for the Family. We knew the previous vicar of the church around the corner. An email or two later, the new vicar and his wife, who had never met us, offered us a parking spot outside their home any time we needed it. Just 100 metres from the hospital's main entrance. This meant Bekah didn't have the task of trying to get me home on the train after my big operation.

Can you hear his rod and his staff?

Then there was the time Prof Hunt said I'd get lymphoedema – a chronic swelling in my leg – after my operation. I'd need to wear a stocking to control it. Bekah knew how much I'd hate this. The thought of wearing a control stocking through the heat of summer was unthinkable. I overheat easily and always sleep with the window open, even in the depths of winter.

'What are the odds of this happening?' Bekah asked.

'It's all but guaranteed to happen with such a big surgery, and having removed so much of his lymphatic system.'

To date, it has never happened. My legs are as shapely as ever, and I've never had to swaddle them. Not once.

Can you hear his rod and his staff?

Then there was Wendy, a good friend. Wendy had a mole on her foot, and it started to morph into something different. Having read my story on Facebook, her daughter nagged her to get it checked out. She did. It was a melanoma, but it was caught in time.

Can you hear his rod and his staff?

Then there was the time I watched TV on my iPad during one of my most tedious sixteen-hour hospital days. Sitting in a chair for hours on end, connected to various drips, it was a long, boring and depressing day. Then a church leader friend, Nigel Bayley, popped up on the small screen along with his mum, winning on *Lingo*, ITV's word-guessing TV quiz. An hour later I was still watching TV when another friend, Suzie Kennedy, appeared as a contestant on *The Chase*. As if that wasn't enough, Angelo, the owner of our favourite Italian restaurant in Hove, arrived at the hospital. The restaurant had closed years back and we hadn't seen him since. He was visiting someone else, but he noticed me and stopped for a chat, a joke and a laugh.

Can you hear his rod and his staff?

Then there was the timing of our visit to Sally on 17 April 2023. When we needed the whole family to be nearby, they were. This was the first time in years that all our girls were resident in West Sussex. Before this, one of them would have been miles away, and sharing the news would have been so much harder. As it was, they were all able to come straight over, and we spent every evening together, talking, crying, laughing and being a family. It was beautiful.

Can you hear his rod and his staff?

At the beginning of this book, I mentioned David Watson, one of the greatest British preachers of the twentieth century. It just so happens that he was diagnosed with terminal cancer. He wrote a book about his journey before he died called *Fear No Evil*. David the preacher was quoting from David the psalmist, as the three words that formed the title of his book were taken from Psalm 23:

Yea, though I walk through the valley of the shadow of death,
I will fear no evil;
For You *are* with me;
Your rod and Your staff, they comfort me.

(Psalm 23:4, NKJV)

David Watson often told the story of a vicar who went on holiday to a remote and mountainous part of the country. He needed to get away to recharge his batteries. As he was walking in the hills, he came across a shepherd boy leading a flock of sheep. The vicar, keen to learn about being a shepherd, stopped and chatted with him. The boy, equally fascinated by the man's profession, asked him to explain what Christianity was about.

'It's like this,' the vicar replied. 'The Bible says, "The Lord is my shepherd." That's from Psalm 23. It's just five words.' Then he raised his right hand and held his fourth finger tightly with his left. 'When a person becomes a Christian, they're able to say, "The Lord is *my* shepherd."' As he said the fourth word, he squeezed the fourth finger of his right hand. 'Can you say that?' he asked.

The boy said he would think about what the vicar had said, and then left to herd his sheep.

The vicar returned a year later and walked the same path in the hope of finding the shepherd boy to continue the discussion, but the boy was nowhere to be seen.

The vicar found a simple house of stone where a woman was

gathering eggs from her chicken house. He stopped and asked if she knew the whereabouts of the boy. The woman's cheerful face suddenly appeared crestfallen.

'Last winter,' she muttered, 'it was bitter. The worst anyone can remember. There were snowdrifts. Blizzards.'

The vicar felt a sense of foreboding.

'My boy tried to rescue some sheep. Got lost. My husband brought him back here when he found him. He was our only son.'

It was the vicar's turn to appear crestfallen. 'I'm so, so sorry,' he said.

'There was something strange about him,' she continued.

'What was that?'

'When they laid my son out, his body was frozen. But his hands were in a very odd position. His left hand was holding the fourth finger of his right hand.' She turned to the vicar and asked, 'Do you have any idea what that might mean?'

The vicar explained that her son had made Jesus his shepherd, and that her boy was now in heaven. They would meet again one day; she could be sure of it.

With that, the vicar spoke God's peace over her, her husband and her house before leaving.

For me, when suffering comes, it's not so much about the why as the where. It's not about asking, *Why is this happening?* It's about asking where God is in it all.

Sometimes, when you're going through a time of darkness and feel a bit lost, all you're going to hear is the sound of the Good Shepherd tapping on the rocks, comforting you with the knowledge that even though you cannot see him, he's there.

All you can do in these situations is hold on to the fourth finger of your right hand and say, 'The Lord is *my* shepherd.'

You'll find Jesus is more than enough. Why? Because:

By embracing death, taking it into himself, he destroyed the

Devil's hold on death and freed all who cower through life, scared to death of death.

(Hebrews 2:15, MSG)

20

I can only imagine

Bekah had done most of the talking when we visited the hospice. I was slightly worried the nurse thought this was some kind of hostage situation, and that my wife wasn't allowing me to speak.

In truth, I didn't know how to express myself coherently. I was too busy trying to swallow the lump in my throat. There was something I did and didn't want to know, in equal measure.

In the end, I plucked up the courage and spoke: 'What happens when you die? I mean, what happens in those last few days and hours?' I just about managed to get the words out before starting to sob.

When I had calmed down, the nurse said, 'There'll be no pain,' she said. 'People become more tired and weak. They sleep a lot. Eventually, they drift off and just don't wake up again.'

As I thought about this later that day, it struck a chord with me. What did Jesus say when he heard that Lazarus had died? He said, 'Our friend Lazarus has fallen asleep; but I am going there to wake him up' (John 11:11).

In Jesus' eyes, it seems that dying is like nodding off and having a decent kip. That doesn't sound too bad, does it? It sounds even better when you remember what he said next: 'I'm going to wake him up.'

If dying is like going to sleep, and death is like being asleep, then resurrection must be like being awoken by Jesus.

The Bible shows us that death is not a hopeless end, but rather an endless hope. I know that's an old cliché, but it's no less true for that. As Christians, we should overflow with hope. Hope is a precious commodity in today's world. People are worried about their future, the future of their children and the future of the world. Many either give in to despair or barely hold it at bay.

We all need hope.

In Hebrews 11:1, the writer says that 'faith is being sure of what we hope for and certain of what we do not see.' That's worth digging into.

Faith isn't passive; it's something active that we do. It is the act of believing in what we cannot yet see. I cannot yet see Jesus face-to-face, but I believe with certainty that he lives, and that he loves me.

He is King of an unshakable kingdom. I believe he died for the wrong things I've done, said and thought, and that he rose again. I believe he ascended into heaven and is seated at the right hand of God. I believe he's coming back on the last day of history, and that he will raise the dead. I believe I will wake up on that day, and I'll see him face to face. That's faith. It's a sure and certain hope that the One I believe in will never forget me.

Today, I believe in Jesus, even though I cannot see him. One day, I will see him because I believe in him. One day, I will be awakened from death like a child from sleep. The first person I will see is Jesus. I only hope I will react better than my children did when I used to wake them up as teenagers!

While many people say, 'I'll believe it when I see it,' the follower of Jesus says, 'I'll see it when I believe it.' This is not just something I *hope for* as a Christian; it's something I *expect*.

What will Jesus look like?

Remember the story that touched Bekah so deeply – the one about Mary Magdalene in John 20? Mary Magdalene went to Jesus' tomb to anoint his dead body. This was a traditional burial custom. On arriving, she saw that the tomb was empty.

When Jesus let her find him, Mary mistook him for the gardener. It was only when he spoke her name that she knew who he really was. She recognised his voice.

I find this fascinating. There was clearly something familiar about Jesus, but also something different. In his resurrection body, Jesus looked like he had before. He sounded like himself, too. Yet there was something about his body that made him look unlike the Jesus that Mary knew.

If this is what happened to Jesus, then presumably I, Steve Legg, will one day look like the Steve Legg you know now. But I will also look different. I will look more alive than I've ever looked. I will look more radiant, more loving, more joyful, more whole. Hard to imagine, I know.

In my new, resurrected body, I will never experience weariness, sickness, sadness or ageing (woohoo!). And the same will be true for my wife, my daughters, my granddaughter and my mates. Everyone.

This is what I believe happens when a follower of Jesus dies. We fall asleep, just as Jesus' friend Lazarus had done. Our bodies are buried or cremated, but our spirits go to a place the Bible calls 'paradise', a word that is commonly translated as 'beautiful garden'. I have always loved watching Alan Titchmarsh and his team make over people's back gardens, but this is next-level horticulture.

I wonder what you would describe as perfect in this life. I know what I would. Being with Bekah. Walking Colbie by the sea. Enjoying meals with my daughters. Holding my granddaughter. Laughing with my mates. When I have these sorts of experiences, it's tempting to use the word Pop Larkin uttered in *The Darling*

Buds of May: 'Perfick!'

Except that it's not 'perfick'. However amazing and life-enhancing these moments are, they are only pale imitations of what's to come. Even my wife Bekah, beautiful and brilliant though she is, is only a shadow of her future self.

So am I.

So are you.

When I think of heaven, all I know is that the Bible tells me it's a place where there is no more pain or crying. I like the sound of that. I imagine it's a place where whatever you imagine to be perfect, based on the goodness of what you've enjoyed in this life, is multiplied to the nth degree.

If 'perfick' for you is walking your dog on the beach, that will be one of the characteristics of heaven for you. Your dog will be even more perfect than he or she was here. The beach will be even more golden. The sea will be even more glorious. The sound of the surf will be a symphony – a heavenly orchestra of harmless winds and waves.

Imagine that.

But the trouble is, we don't. The Bible tells us we should set our hearts and minds on the things that are above where Jesus is, but we don't. We are too focused on the things of this earth. Until, that is, we are told we only have five months to live. Then we re-evaluate.

We start to seek first the unshakeable kingdom of God. We start to fix our eyes more intently on Jesus. He becomes the first thought in our hearts and the first name on our lips. Why? Because heaven is Jesus, and Jesus is heaven. And there's nothing or no one more important than that.

Epilogue

I know some of you will be wanting a proper ending to this book, but at the time of writing this epilogue I haven't been miraculously healed, nor have I been called home.

In fact, I've just come back from a lovely stroll along the beach with my wonderful pal David Thatcher. David is a long-standing, faithful friend who has picked me up every week and taken me and the dog out. He always insists on buying the coffee and getting me a cheeky almond croissant.

I'm feeling really well. Apart from the insulin for my diabetes, I'm on no medication at all – not even an aspirin.

So this is a story, in a sense, with an open ending. All I can tell you is what the latest medical report says. We've just had a call from the doctor. They haven't received the CT results yet, so they can't comment on what's happening in my body, but the MRI shows that the two remaining marks in my brain (there were thirteen in May) have shrunk. This is very positive news, and certainly something to celebrate – particularly as nothing new has appeared. This represents a huge answer to many prayers.

If you're one of the people who has been praying, Bekah and I want to thank you.

What, then, does the future hold?

The honest answer is, I don't know.

All I do know is that God is with me.

People sometimes ask, 'What has God been saying to you through all this?'

'Three things,' I reply. 'He's saying, "I love you. I'm with you. Try not to be scared."'

Those are such reassuring and comforting words, because it can be scary living with a terminal diagnosis.

'It's a death sentence,' some say.

'I disagree,' I respond. 'I'm not under a sentence of death. I'm under a sentence of life. Being told I only have five months to live has made me more determined than ever to do what Jesus wants us all to do: live life in all its fullness (John 10:10) and share the good news with as many as I can.'

And that's what Bekah and I have tried to do. I firmly believe we're in a win-win situation. If I'm healed, I get to live many more years with my family and friends, doing the things Jesus has called me to do, and living my life with a greater sense of priority and a reduced level of pressure.

If I die, I get to go to heaven. I get to be with Jesus. I get to walk with him on sunny sands.

At the beginning of this book, I talked about *The Shawshank Redemption*. I talked about the choices we all face every day, whether we have cancer or not.

We can get busy living, or we can get busy dying. We can get busy laughing, or we can get busy crying. I've chosen to get busy living. I've chosen to make sure I have the last laugh, even in the face of death.

The Shawshank Redemption is a film about hope. Those who give up on hope in Shawshank prison give up on life. Hope is what keeps the prisoners alive – especially Andy and his pal Red.

It is hope that motivates Andy to escape from jail, and it is hope that keeps Red going until the point when he is finally released by the parole board.

In the end, it is hope that propels Red to find the buried box Andy has left for him in a field – a box containing everything Red needs to seek and find his friend. When he does, it is on a sandy beach beside the Pacific Ocean, unimaginably blue.

As he walks towards Andy, who is mending an old fishing boat near the surf, the smile on Red's face and the love in his eyes are as bright as the blazing sun. They have both found their heart's true home, beside an ocean that Andy describes as a warm place with no memory.

This sounds like heaven to me.

I may end up walking on the seafront in L.A. with my dog for many more years. Or I may end up walking with my best friend Jesus beside an ocean that is bluer than the Pacific, on sand made from grains of gold.

Who knows?

God does.

And that's a thought that makes me happy.

So happy, I am laughing.

God, you did everything you promised, and I'm thanking you with all my heart. You pulled me from the brink of death, my feet from the cliff-edge of doom. Now I stroll at leisure with God in the sunlit fields of life.

(Psalm 56:12-13, MSG)

OTHER BOOKS BY STEVE LEGG

Making Friends: Evangelism the easy way
Man, Myth or Maybe More
Big Questions
The A-Z of Evangelism
Firm Foundations
The A-Z of Christmas
The Chancer

BOOKS STEVE WROTE WITH ALEXA TEWKESBURY

It's a Boy!
Lions, Whales and Thrilling Tales
The Lying Tree
cyberSky

BOOKS STEVE WROTE WITH BEKAH LEGG

All Together
Life Together
Time Together
Growing Together
Advent Together

NEVER MISS A COPY
WHEN YOU
SUBSCRIBE TO SORTED

Come on.
Do it now.
Get Sorted.

HOUSE
of
DREAMS

MARK STIBBE

Another magical tale by award-winning
author, Mark Stibbe.

Available in paperback
and eBook on Amazon.

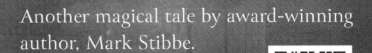

MEN'S HEALTH MATTERS PODCAST

With Steve Legg & Dr Ken

LISTEN TO THIS PODCAST ON: